BLOOD ON CHINA BEACH

My Story as a Brain Surgeon in Vietnam

Paul J. Pitlyk

iUniverse, Inc.
Bloomington

Blood on China Beach
My Story as a Brain Surgeon in Vietnam

Copyright © 2012, 2013 Paul J. Pitlyk

All rights reserved. No part of this book may be used or reproduced by any means, graphic, electronic, or mechanical, including photocopying, recording, taping or by any information storage retrieval system without the written permission of the publisher except in the case of brief quotations embodied in critical articles and reviews.

iUniverse books may be ordered through booksellers or by contacting:

iUniverse
1663 Liberty Drive
Bloomington, IN 47403
www.iuniverse.com
1-800-Authors (1-800-288-4677)

Because of the dynamic nature of the Internet, any Web addresses or links contained in this book may have changed since publication and may no longer be valid. The views expressed in this work are solely those of the author and do not necessarily reflect the views of the publisher, and the publisher hereby disclaims any responsibility for them.

Any people depicted in stock imagery provided by Thinkstock are models, and such images are being used for illustrative purposes only.

Certain stock imagery © Thinkstock.

ISBN: 978-1-4759-5943-7 (sc)
ISBN: 978-1-4759-5945-1 (hc)
ISBN: 978-1-4759-5944-4 (e)

Library of Congress Control Number: 2012920798

Printed in the United States of America

iUniverse rev. date: 3/14/2013

To Nicole

I would remind you again how large and various was the experience of the battlefield and how fertile the blood of warriors in rearing good surgeons.
—Sir Clifford Allbutt (1836–1925),
University of Cambridge

Contents

1. The Wall — 1
2. A Time of Discontentment — 6
3. Decision — 11
4. Journey to Nam — 18
5. Alien World — 31
6. Charlie Med — 42
7. Toil and Trouble — 51
8. Settling In — 66
9. China Beach — 83
10. Supply and Demand — 103
11. Bloody Spring — 117
12. The Commander — 128
13. Between Darkness and Light — 141
14. Noble Attempts — 156
15. Combat — 171
16. Summer Heat — 188
17. Mission of Mercy — 205
18. Winding Down — 220
19. Separation Anxiety — 230

Prologue

It was a rainy November night at Charlie Med, a primitive forward aid station in the jungle outside Da Nang. It was 1965, and I was a young newly trained brain surgeon who'd given up the easy life in suburban Midwest America to voluntarily serve my country in Vietnam. My friends thought I was crazy to want to go, but something deep inside compelled me. I wanted to find myself, I guess, and I wasn't making much progress. As the rain beat down on the roof of my tent, I let my mind wander back over my life. What had brought me here? What really had made me want to come? Why was I so unhappy in traditional America? Why was I so unfulfilled?

Suddenly, I heard the now-familiar sound of approaching choppers. I tensed. Choppers at Charlie Med meant wounded were coming in. I left my tent and watched as the landing lights of the helicopters lit up our landing pad. I sighed and shook my head. The first chopper came in. Another followed. Then a third, fourth, and fifth arrived. In total, twenty casualties were on board, and now they were ours.

Their injuries were varied, including the three wounded marines with brain injuries that resulted from exploding hand grenades, land mines, or the infamous Bouncing Betty, a particularly hideous booby trap that could cut a soldier in half. All three needed cranial surgery. But the time required for brain operations was lengthy. Several other marines with chest and abdominal trauma also required early surgery, and these men had a much higher probability of survival and recovery. Triage meant my guys had to wait. I was not allocated an operating room; rather, I could use it only if available. My only choice was to do as I occasionally did at Charlie Med. I called to the corpsmen to carry my marines into a nearby dirty tent. They got them inside and heaved the most seriously wounded man off the stretcher and onto a bloodstained picnic table.

"Hold the light closer!" I said, my voice charged with urgency as I began inspecting the wound. The corpsman holding the flashlight moved closer.

I was operating quite literally with nothing beyond the most basic tools as artillery boomed in the near distance, and the sound of rifle fire carried over the pounding rain. I had no anesthesiologist, anesthesia, reasonable surgical instruments, sterility, or bright light. My two assistants meant well, but they were ineffective. A strong gust of wind shook the tent, causing the thing to almost breathe in and out. Blood-soaked mud covered my jungle boots, the lower half of my surgical gown, and much of my shirt. The entire place stunk of mildew, blood, human waste, and smells I couldn't identify.

Although the patient was essentially comatose, he occasionally groaned and wiggled as I began to operate, causing further problems. Using a small bottle of local anesthetic, I injected the scalp around the penetration site. He quieted a bit, and I proceeded. With a scalpel, I opened the wound wider to access the skull. Then using a rongeur, I opened the skull adjacent to the penetration area, and brain tissue under pressure from swelling oozed out along with blood and dripped to the mud beneath us. Using a crude aspiration system, I attempted to clear the area of blood and crushed brain.

As I worked, more and more swollen brain matter came out of the man's head. His brain looked like gray-white toothpaste collecting in twirled solid tubes. It was as if some evil troll was pushing the brain out of the hole from the inside. As I struggled to stop the bleeding and relieve the pressure inside the marine's head, I wondered what the hell I was doing twelve thousand miles from home in the middle of a bloody war.

1

THE WALL

THE WALL. THAT'S WHAT IT'S CALLED, even though the official name for it is the Vietnam Veterans Memorial. The polished black granite glistened even in the subdued gray light filtering down from an overcast sky as I stood looking at the names etched into the stone. So many names. So many dead brave Americans. In all, there were 58,195 etchings artfully and simply carved on the expanse of mirror-like darkness, though over the years more names have been added, bringing the total to 58,272. Glancing to my right, I took in the spear of the Washington Monument to the east. The Lincoln Memorial rose to the west, and I reflected on the apparently diminutive nature of the Memorial Wall in comparison to the grand monuments around the National Mall.

The Vietnam Veterans Memorial was not without controversy. It was not supposed to be a war memorial, but rather a site dedicated to the memory of all who served in Vietnam, not just those who died there. Some said Maya Ying Lin's concept of making the memorial a park within a park was not sufficiently honoring the bravery of our soldiers, while others thought it was just the right thing to do. The Wall had just been dedicated a week or so before my visit, opening to the public in a somber ceremony on November 13, 1982. So it was all new to me and everyone else at the time. I was one of the first of millions of visitors to come see it. For me, the Wall was special, haunting, and not a little disturbing because of the memories it summoned.

I'd come to Washington, DC, not expressly to see the Wall, though there was some odd connection between the two I didn't quite comprehend at the time. I was in town for a meeting about a proposal by the Bureau of Medicine and Surgery within the navy to withdraw neurosurgeons from the battlefield position to a much better equipped facility well back from the front lines. Since I had experience working as a brain surgeon under terrible conditions in the jungles of Vietnam, my input was sought.

A bunch of other neurosurgeons with similar experience had come together in committee fashion to weigh the advantages and disadvantages of this proposal, and either concur with the idea or make a counter proposal to the navy. Over the previous two days I had been confined in a meeting room of a local hotel for eight hours each day, during which time all of the ramifications and implications of such a proposal were discussed in detail and either supported or challenged by those in attendance.

The forward position, known as an Echelon II facility, manages emergency surgery. It has limited capabilities and is crude. Care, however, is rapidly delivered. The Echelon III surgical facility is well equipped, well staffed, and provides very good care. It, however, is often hours from the battlefield. Brain injuries cannot tolerate delayed surgery, making it unwise to move the neurosurgeons away from the battlefield. I was in favor of keeping neurosurgeons in Echelon II facilities, and I repeatedly said so.

When the meetings finally ended, I had some time to kill, and I found myself drawn inexorably to view the Vietnam Veterans Memorial. I couldn't go home without seeing it. As I stood in front of the Wall, I realized that the place held great meaning for me, and I was emotionally unprepared. It was a private and pristine recess and in no way ostentatious.

At the top of the shallow column of stairs stood a pedestal crowned with a broad thick book that looked like a medieval Bible. This large text was enclosed in a weather-shielding glass case affording protection from the elements on the sides and the top. One could access the book, however, by opening the hinged glass cover and perusing the pages. The book contained literally thousands of names arranged alphabetically.

I shivered and drew my coat closer. The temperature was about thirty-five degrees, and the wind coming off of the nearby Potomac River was kicking up. Dead leaves brushed by my face as I studied the book, transfixed as my memory drifted back through the years to a place fifteen thousand miles from this spot. The scene reunited me with many of the names I recognized and recalled as I turned the pages of this large parchment-like bound tome. The cold wind and gray winter day were erased from my mind as my eyes drifted slowly from name to name. I remembered the seeming futility of trying to operate on kids out in a jungle forward aid station, and how I felt when I'd first arrived in-country. I'd performed my surgeries to the best of my ability, only to lose yet another good man.

I continued to follow my freezing and admittedly trembling finger as it traced the names over many pages, and I occasionally recognized one more. Then another. I'd picture the gaping head wounds, the burns, the stumps where legs and arms had once been. Then, whether it was the inclement weather, the increasing chill, the whistling wind in the bare trees, or a still scarred and unhealed emotion, a new horrific picture was painted in my mind. I began to shudder. The horror and the madness loomed clear in my memory once again.

Turning from the huge reference book and looking directly at the Wall, I saw that a few tourists had wandered down the steps to gaze upon the black shining inscribed surface. Approaching the Wall within inches, they were scanning for names. Several minutes later a woman in her thirties came by with a young girl about ten or eleven years old. They walked down the steps to the Wall, searched a short while for a particular name, and then turned slowly away. Holding her daughter's hand, the woman came back up the stairs. As they walked by me, the young girl asked, "Won't Daddy get cold down there?"

I had had enough. Washington, with its marvelous monuments and reams of history—the heart of American government and society—was for a short period entirely negated in my mind. It was diminished because of this disturbing encounter and a vivid reminder of an imperishable mental record that I knew I would have for the remainder of my days.

I walked off the path, exiting the monument, which was lined with winter-bare trees, the cold, biting wind whistling through their branches. Again, fallen leaves swirled up by the gusty wind frequently bounced off my face, thus preventing me from becoming so distracted that I would wander aimlessly.

I proceeded to the edge of the Mall, found a taxicab, and went directly back to my hotel. It was late afternoon, and with little else to do, I lay down on the bed in my room.

Hearing nothing save the sounds of the gentle hum of the heating system, I grew drowsy. I rolled over on my side, looked out the window, and saw again nothing but gray overcast and dark-colored buildings in the distance.

Ironically, my window was positioned such that in the distance one could look across the city and see the brightly lit dome of the US Capitol. I was struck by the fact that the monument that moved me so much was not even visible. In fact, it was well below the treetops of the rows of trees on the Mall. All that's important was sinking away. I lay back, stared directly at the ceiling, and felt my eyes growing heavy, although I had no intention of sleeping for several hours yet. The emotional experience of the riveting afternoon consumed my energy, though. I tried to resist falling asleep, but I was emotionally drained from my experience at the Vietnam Veterans Memorial. I fell into a deep sleep.

And the dream came again. It was one of many dreams I had that brought me back to when I was only thirty-two and a fledgling neurosurgeon in the midst of war. The horror of young vibrant marines turned into raw meat jolted me awake in a cold sweat.

A Time of Discontentment

AT TIMES, EVERY PERSON MUST FACE the proverbial fork in the road, or a time of indecision that is bad for the soul. I was in such a time early in 1965. I was within days of finishing my residency training as a neurosurgeon at the Mayo Clinic. Every day I wondered where I would go and what I would do with this newly acquired capability of something called neurologic surgery.

Although I had spent over five years at the Mayo Clinic learning the various nuances of neuroanatomy, neurophysiology, and neuropathology, I lacked the all-important hands-on experience that imparts the hand-eye coordination, the earmark of an adept surgeon.

Although during my years at the Mayo Clinic I was exposed to and learned quite accurately the didactics of this relatively obscure division of surgery, this hands-on experience was a major shortfall at that institution. The reason is quite simple. Patients come from great distances and spend a great deal of money to go to the institution for what they perceive as the ultimate in medical and surgical care. Such patients rightfully thought they deserved only the best surgeons, which made on-the-job training of a new surgeon like me somewhat problematic.

Although I felt competent in those aspects of the field of neurosurgery that did not include actual operations on patients—namely, the evaluation and diagnosis of neurosurgical diseases, the examination of the patient, and the various radiologic and electrodiagnostic tests that were required—the day I completed training and left to seek a private practice of my own, I could not "operate"! I was very well aware of my lack of confidence in myself as a surgeon at the time, and I believe to this day that I was right to feel as I did.

At the time I completed my training, I had achieved everything I set out to do in my life, and yet I felt a sense of insecurity and loneliness, much like a metaphorical ship without a rudder. I had interviews with a few interested neurosurgeons seeking an associate. Unlike the four other young men with whom I trained, I failed to make a commitment and, thus, at the completion of my program had made no arrangements for a professional position. I was thirty-two and emotionally drifting. I simply tossed my few belongings in the trunk of my car, filled the tank with gasoline, and with less than two hundred dollars to my name, left the city of Rochester on a bitter cold January morning in 1965. I started driving through southern Minnesota and then crossed over the Mississippi River into the state of Wisconsin, heading toward Chicago.

The countryside was winter bleak. The sun had not shone for weeks, and woods were covered with snow. The temperature hovered in the twenties.

After driving several hours, I found myself on the outskirts of Milwaukee, Wisconsin, and elected to stay there for the night. After checking into a motel and having something to eat, I went to my room and wondered whether a position was available in this city. I then opened a local *Yellow Pages*, went to "physicians," and then looked for the subheading of "neurological surgeons." I called one and inquired about a job.

As chance would have it, this individual was just one year older than me, had been in practice about one year, and indeed was looking for a partner.

We met the next day, talked, and discussed the merits of the practice (trauma versus elective cases), financial considerations, etc. Then we agreed upon a professional relationship and proceeded to complete the necessary paperwork.

I rented a furnished efficiency apartment and moved in my belongings, which were easily absorbed in about half of one closet. Shortly thereafter, I went out and bought a new car—a convertible. I assumed this notion was designed to fit the image of a flowering, if only embryonic, career—insecure as I was!

The next several days included meeting my new partner's office staff, applying to the staff of the three local hospitals where he maintained his practice, and meeting multiple physicians at the various facilities. Together we began seeing patients, responding to consultations from the hospital and emergency rooms, and embarking upon the traditional private practice of neurosurgery.

A low rumbling, however, was mounting deep in my mind. I felt unhappy, unfulfilled, and insecure. Ironically, the news on the radio and in the newspapers was beginning to echo a brewing and slowly expanding military conflict in far-off South Vietnam.

For reasons that were not immediately obvious to me, I found myself seeking more information about this growing conflict. Meanwhile, I continued methodically and in a

Pavlovian fashion, discharging the daily responsibility of a neurosurgeon in a community environment, with its attendant responsibilities of not only evaluating and carrying out surgery albeit with a sense of anxiety over insecurity, but additionally meeting more and more potential referring physician sources, attending the traditional cocktail parties, and increasing my potential exposure so as to attract more and more referrals. I was gradually becoming mired in a class system, which included a strata I found progressively repulsive.

For five years I had trained, often day and night, to ultimately arrive at this point in my life, a spot in this world where most men would be delighted (personal, financial, and professional success guaranteed). I was not content. More and more, the news from Southeast Asia dominated the networks and the newspapers, curiously mesmerizing my thinking. This news acted as my potential escape from the social quagmire into which I was beginning to become entangled.

Certain events from my younger years were clearly intertwined and operative in the development of my growing anxiety. Not the least of these was the fact that I had grown up in a family where, as a young boy, I saw three older brothers enter the military and go to the South Pacific in the course of the Second World War. Additionally, my father had served in the First World War in France and often reminisced. Indeed, a younger brother entered the military during my college years and returned as a veteran before I had even graduated from medical school.

One evening late in my medical education, while sitting in the living room of our home, my father looked at the wall covered with portraits of each of his sons in their uniforms. Then he turned to me and said, "Paul, do you think you will ever be good enough to be on the wall?"

Driven partly by this parental rejection and an additional poorly understood array of motivating factors, I found myself yearning for an escape from this confined, labyrinthine environment that many young men would give their all to have.

Maybe something about the confining discipline of training had left me ill equipped to enter into civilian practice. Maybe not. In any case, a mounting sense of nationalism, excitement, and adventure, with its inherent risks, plus a sense of insecurity and a desire to run tempted me to contact the medical department of the navy in Washington, DC.

Why the navy? I haven't the slightest idea.

For the next few weeks I convinced myself that this was both foolish and dangerous. The notion was abandoned. Whatever this underlying emotional process was, however, it could not be extinguished. For many days I would think about the call—and then stop short. The back-and-forth cycle began to drive me crazy, but I buried my inner turmoil, or at least I tried to. In the meantime, the practice continued: office consultations, elective surgery, and more structured entertainment to meet additional doctors. I met and worked with several physicians for whom I had the highest professional and personal respect. Although I wanted to, I never shared my mental conflict with my partner or anyone else.

Yet, I could not escape from my feelings. I was emotionally torn by the conflict between what I should be doing and what I was contemplating. The gnawing, unquenchable need to give up everything I had worked so hard to achieve and strike out into the unknown persisted. In retrospect, I think the risk and danger, and the possibility that I might die in the war, motivated me more than I admitted to myself at the time.

3

DECISION

THE DAY OF MY DECISION REMAINS vivid to me even now, so many years later. It was about two o'clock in the afternoon while I was sitting at my desk in our medical office building. I assured myself that the door to the secretary's office was closed. Then after obtaining the phone number through the long distance information operator, I was able to contact Captain Black, the medical program director for the navy. He answered the phone in a polite yet direct fashion, identifying himself and his position.

I stated my name and indicated that I had recently completed a residency in neurosurgery and was in private practice but was interested in joining the navy, specifically for the purpose of being assigned to a position with maximum need and excitement and with no particular regard to location.

There was a hesitation on the part of Captain Black for at least thirty seconds. In fact, I thought for a moment he hung up the phone. However, he had not, and when he did respond, he asked, "Are you for real?"

I continued that I was and that I was sincere in my intent.

He then said rather abruptly, "Give me your social security number, and wait at that phone for thirty minutes."

I provided the number and hung up the phone. Well within the thirty minutes, the phone rang, and it was indeed Captain Black, indicating an avowed interest and advising me to proceed promptly to a navy recruiting office in Milwaukee for processing into the navy as a lieutenant.

Following this phone conversation, I had the feeling that I had gone to confession and been absolved of every egregious crime that I had ever committed. A sense of vindication and exhilaration displaced all anxiety. My self-respect was dramatically enhanced, and my attitude toward colleagues and acquaintances was measurably improved.

Embarrassed as I am to admit my frailties, human nature began to overcome me, and a fear for my well-being overcame this decision. I therefore failed to contact the Milwaukee Navy Recruiting Office. In fact, three weeks went by when again, in the middle of an afternoon while seeing patients in my office, the phone rang and it was Captain Black from the navy, wondering about the status of my application. I quickly manufactured a response, indicating that I had been quite busy with surgery and would be getting to the matter within the next few days.

Following this call, an element of shame, embarrassment, and cowardice began to cloud my mind and influence my personal interactions with others. I suspect my determination and courage had been shaken. I waited one more week and then drove to the recruiting office in downtown Milwaukee, identified myself to the young ensign in charge, and said I wanted to apply for a commission as a medical officer in the navy.

To my mild surprise, he responded, "We have been waiting for you, sir."

The next several weeks were pleasant and enjoyable. I had consummated my decision and was no longer living with a disturbed mind-set. The navy continued processing my application while I simply discharged my responsibilities as a fledgling neurosurgeon. My decision was shared with several of my colleagues with whom I had grown close in this short period in Milwaukee. I was most gratified that, although surprised, the reactions of all save one were positive.

One of the physicians (obviously a vet of WWII) commented, "You will never have to explain to anyone where you were in time of national conflict."

The single detractor was an ophthalmologist in my office building who, when he heard of my decision, was stunned to a mild level of irritation. He said, "With a stroke of the pen, you have sacrificed sixteen years of intense education and a potentially marvelous career!"

It is my perception, however, that life is like a diamond with many facets. Most of us see the world through only one of these facets. Although I had trouble identifying my proper facet, I had found it now and was not letting go! For me, for reasons not fully apparent, there was only one direction, and I would not alter course. My friend and well-meaning ophthalmologist then, and to this day more than forty-five years later, was unequivocally wrong!

I was immersed in a luxurious cloud of relief, satisfaction, enchantment, and flag-waving patriotism. My girlfriend, Alice, a nurse in Milwaukee, tried to understand why I'd made such a potentially life-changing or even fatal decision, yet in the end I don't think she ever really did. After all, I didn't really understand the full extent of my motivation to do this.

It took about a month to extricate myself from the practice of neurosurgery in Milwaukee, which included shifting my professional responsibilities to a partner (who had just recovered from a significant heart attack and was now ready to go back to work). Meanwhile, the navy was processing my commission.

I presented my notice to vacate my apartment and continued to practice, finishing out the final few weeks upon which I had agreed. I was contacted by one of my sisters in St. Louis, who wondered whether I was in trouble with the federal government since the FBI had been asking the neighbors questions regarding me. Evidently such a background investigation is carried out by the FBI on any individual who applies for a commission in the armed services.

Thus, officials systematically contact friends, neighbors, and professional associates, looking for any suggested integrity or security breach. All this is done in the course of a background check.

I informed my sister of my plans and that I would be returning to St. Louis shortly for only a brief visit. Since my parents were advancing in age, it was my intent to advise them that I was going into the navy and would be assigned to a hospital in Hawaii for two years. Thus, I planned to deflect any concern they might have about my well-being. My sisters and brothers agreed that this was an appropriate thing to do and cooperated in this deception.

With all details completed in Milwaukee and my brief stay there over, I departed. The drive to St. Louis was about six hours, so I had time to both reflect and anticipate. The concerns about my technical adequacy in the operating room were only partly eased during my brief surgical career in Milwaukee. Indeed, in one particular situation, I was removing a brain tumor from a woman and, because I was not technically adept, the blood loss during the operation was significantly greater than would be experienced by a surgeon of greater competence. In actual fact, I used eight units of blood during the operation and still was not finished. One of the nurses in the operating room advised me that there was no more blood of the type required by this woman left in the hospital. Obviously this further heightened my anxiety. I envisioned this woman dying while I moved with desperation. My heart pounded and my hands trembled, yet with fortunate hand movements, I was able to complete the operation without the need for a ninth unit. We were both very lucky.

The drive to St. Louis was pleasant on that October afternoon. My plans were galvanized. I was at peace with myself. Once I arrived home I was greeted by my parents and, over subsequent days, visited siblings, their families, and several friends from early school years. I then went about the business of selling my automobile, now only a few months old, and I contacted the St. Louis Navy Recruiting Office for continuation and completion of my matriculation into the navy. A curious thing happened when I drove my nearly new convertible to a used auto dealer and offered it for sale. His comment was "What's the matter, buddy? Can't you keep up the payments?"

I said, "That's life."

Finally, the day came when I was to report to the main recruiting office in the downtown part of St. Louis to be sworn in, an experience that I relished. Following the event, they provided me with an airline ticket and a set of orders to report to the marine base at Camp Pendleton, California. In the few days before leaving, I saw a great deal of my friends and my brothers and sisters, most of whom were married and lived in the environs of St. Louis.

The day of departure, I maintained a convincing and

lighthearted attitude for my parents and one of my sisters at home that day. The sister, of course, complemented this emotional frivolity in the presence of my parents and expressed her envy, exclaiming how fortunate I was to be going to such a beautiful place in the world for the next year or so.

I hugged my mother and shook hands with my father. I could tell he was quite proud of the fact that another one of his sons would now serve in the military. My sister drove me to Lambert Field, the St. Louis airport. Her attitude was somber. I told her I was not going to be out in the bush with fighting troops and doubted I would ever hear gunfire. She waited with me in the departure lounge for the airline agent to call for boarding. We spoke in a very sincere, open, and non-emotional manner. I truly was enthusiastic about this venture, and it was apparent in my manner.

The gate agent called for boarding. However, we sat and talked some more while most of the passengers boarded the plane. I then stood up, hugged her, and told her again that this was what I wanted to do and that someone else would do the shooting. She asked that I do one thing before I leave the country.

I asked, "What is that?"

"Have your picture taken in your uniform, and send it home before you leave the country. It will be very important to Dad."

I agreed, turned, walked down the passageway toward the airliner, turned once more, and waved to her. Then I disappeared into the plane. At that moment, for the first time since I had agreed to go, a sinister sense of fear began to enshroud me. I was surprised and embarrassed that this feeling arose, but it was quite real.

The plane pushed back away from the gate and then crept slowly along the ramp, moved out onto the active runway, and accelerated. Though I was fearful at the time I volunteered, the reality of personal risk was rammed home with great force when that airplane started to crawl. A cold sweat developed when I realized finality was clearly a possibility. I was scared!

4

JOURNEY TO NAM

THE FLIGHT FROM ST. LOUIS TO Los Angeles was about four hours. I was sitting in a seat next to a relatively young woman who, after thirty minutes or so into the flight, began talking to me.

Shortly, I became absorbed in the conversation and was able to dismiss the sense of fear that had befallen me at the time of departure. As we talked, she inquired about what I did in this world, and we discussed that for a short period. She then asked why I was going to Los Angeles, so I told her. She seemed quite stunned and sat silent for several minutes before she attempted to reengage in conversation.

Curiously, the sense of fear that I had an hour or so earlier had subsided, and I sensed by her voice and mannerisms it had been transferred to her. How strange, she didn't even know me! I continued the conversation and unintentionally projected an indifferent, nonchalant attitude, which in fact is precisely how I was feeling.

When she again spoke, she sounded surprised and somewhat frightened. In some ways it was the expression of a person walking the last mile with a convict, heading to the electric chair. She spoke of her family and her husband, who was retired from the navy. For a while she did not want to discuss Vietnam in any way, shape, or fashion. I believe her curiosity overcame her in time, however, and she inquired as to the quality of the facilities in Vietnam for carrying out the surgery I was trained to do. I told her honestly I did not know but did not expect anything elaborate. The conversation lapsed to the mundane. She, however, returned to the major topic and focused on the growing menace in Vietnam and the increased number of Americans becoming involved. I began to suspect that she probably had not seen or talked to a person up to this point who was directly involved in that conflict.

The flight passed rather quickly, and we began descending into Los Angeles. As we departed the plane, I told her it was nice to have met her. Then, as I turned to walk away, I saw on her face an expression not unlike that of my sister in St. Louis just a few hours earlier. She looked worried, and I again thought it a little odd that a complete stranger would feel that way about me.

I proceeded on, flying to San Diego, and after getting off the plane I contacted a marine liaison desk in the airport, showed my orders to the sergeant, and was advised to get on a military shuttle vehicle that would take me from the airport up the coast to Oceanside, California, and the Camp Pendleton Marine Base. I made my way to the shuttle, as directed, and when it left for the base I sat looking out the window at nothing in particular. The woman on the plane lingered in my mind. Although I no longer felt scared, I did wonder if I had signed on for something that might turn out to be a little more intense than I'd envisioned. I knew nothing about war, except from what my Dad and older brothers had shared with us. Nobody can know war without experiencing it firsthand, and that idea made me wonder if I was ready for the challenges ahead.

A while later, we drove through the main gate. All around me the base sprawled out, a semiarid wasteland of rolling hills filled with brush and very few trees. The terrain was dotted here and there with larger two-story and small yellow-orange frame buildings, each with a stenciled number on it, presumably to identify its location and function on some central map of the base.

It took some time for the vehicle to work its way into the "main side" area of the reservation. This was an assemblage of primitive buildings. There were one- and two-story yellow frame buildings, each with a different number on the side. The streets were without curbs, and the landscape around the buildings was arid, scattered brush and unkempt. As I was to learn, it was laid out with the monotonous symmetry of most military installations. I was taken to a building where incoming personnel went through an administrative indoctrination process. I handed my orders to a marine officer at a certain desk and then was referred to an adjacent desk for naval personnel. I then stood around for an hour or so while busy people in uniform were writing on forms, stamping others with rubber stamps, duplicating papers, and interacting with both me and others in a strictly indifferent fashion, a manner I later found to be so typical in the military.

Finally, I was given an assigned officer's housing location and advised of the location of the uniform shop for procuring uniforms and having them tailored accordingly. I was then told the location of the food hall, commonly referred to in the Marine Corps as the "chow hall," and advised to show up, after I had acquired a uniform at still another building for several days of schooling in "combat medicine."

Finally, the officer behind the desk handed me my set

of processed orders and instructed me to go out the front door and get into a waiting marine vehicle with a driver who would take me to my room at the officers' housing building. I did as I was told and headed outside. I got into the jeep, and as we drove, the driver recognized that I was brand-new to the service and advised that when I wanted to go anywhere on the base, I could simply go to a telephone in the officers' housing area, call a certain number, and a driver and a vehicle would appear at the door within twenty or so minutes to take me hither and there on the base.

The system worked well. After dropping my bags off in the cold-appearing room in another yellow frame building and meeting my roommate, we called for a vehicle to go to the chow hall, where the food was certainly adequate yet not overly appealing. After another phone call, another vehicle appeared and we were taken back to our housing complex. The next day after still another phone call, I was taken to the uniform center, where I was fitted with a navy officer's summer uniform and, of course, the khaki field uniforms that are worn most of the time. After this, another phone call took me to the building where the combat medical school was already in session for approximately two weeks of the four for which it was scheduled.

I found a chair and sat in the crowded classroom. It consisted of about sixty people—doctors, dentists, chaplains, and corpsmen—all listening to various navy and marine officers talking about what we could expect to see in Vietnam, including the climate, the wildlife, the terrain, the threat, and the like. Over the next few days, we were shown the type of tents we would be living in and working out of. While showing us a sleeping tent, the marine jokingly said the tent would hold eight officers or thirty-five enlisted men. We all laughed. We were made familiar with the various weapons that marines use and were taken to ranges where both riflemen and machine gun crews were firing these weapons. This was my first contact with the intense noise of warfare. Clearly it was impressive! We were then transported to another location, where we were instructed on the use of a .45-caliber pistol that would be our personal weapon while in Vietnam. Included were instructions on how to assemble and disassemble this thing, how to clean it, and then finally we were driven to a range and taught to fire the weapon.

I distinctly recall a curious anecdote in this phase of our training. One of the navy officers in the school was a Catholic priest who, like me, was new to the navy but indeed was now a navy chaplain. When ordered to fire the weapon by the marine officer in charge, he said that he was supposed to be a noncombatant and he didn't think it was appropriate. The deeply tanned, trim marine officer in charge very bluntly said to the priest, "Father! Where you are going the enemy does not distinguish between combatants and noncombatants. They would be delighted to kill you."

The priest hesitated and then quietly responded, "I guess you're right. It's a good idea that I at least learn something about this thing."

As I recall, he fired off several rounds and was quite accurate with this sidearm, to the amazement of all of us.

We continued the daily routine of this schooling process. The training included continued use of the hand weapon on the firing range, and further instruction into what to expect in Vietnam, including mock field activities and detailed instruction as to what medical supplies would be available to us and an illustration of same. Finally, there was a demonstration of an armored amphibious vehicle, which is a large tracked vehicle that looked something like a tank but is carried on a ship up to a point several hundred yards off a beach. Then it is lowered off a back ramp from the vessel and loaded with marines. It actually swims through the surf to shore, climbs on the beach, and then moves inland, shielding the troops from small-arms fire. At a certain point inland, the landing craft opens a large front ramp that falls directly downward, and the marines assault the beach.

This was a huge behemoth, easily eight or nine feet above the sandy beach and about twenty-two or twenty-three feet long. The marine driver opened the ramp-like front door through which we entered and instructed us to sit on the bench-like structures. The drawbridge-like ramp was then drawn up. When the door is closed, one is cast into complete darkness, which I found somewhat unnerving. Then the big diesel engine started, and the whole contraption shook, rattled, roared, and smelled like the tailpipe of a city bus. The driver, who was perched on a pedestal-like seat in the front left of the vehicle, sat higher than the passengers, looking forward through a small periscope.

As I recall, the machine had no steering wheel but rather two vertical levers side by side that came up between the driver's legs whereby he could steer. Apparently, pulling the lever on the right stopped the track on the right and, thus, caused the vehicle to turn to the right, while the left lever stopped the left track and caused the vehicle to turn to the left. Pulling them both would obviously stop the machine. I do not know how they backed it up.

Each of us was allowed to drive it along the beach; however, the marines felt it was unwise to take it out in the ocean with a load of physicians and chaplains. I did not contest this decision made by the marine officer in charge. I was impressed that this monster could swim.

After approximately two weeks of our training, we were told that we had graduated, including me, who arrived halfway through the course. No gowns, no diplomas, no grades. We were provided with a set of orders and airline tickets, and we were expected at Travis Air Force Base in Northern California approximately five days hence for travel directly to Saigon, Vietnam. During this four-or five-day hiatus, I had a picture taken in uniform, as requested by my sister, and sent it directly to my father in St. Louis.

There was a navy neurosurgeon at the naval hospital in nearby San Diego, who I had known and become friends with while I was a resident at the Mayo Clinic. So my first night off I went down to San Diego, about thirty-five miles south of Camp Pendleton, and visited with him and his family. He carefully reviewed my orders, since he was very familiar with the navy and advised me that I would be working with the Marine Corps for the next year somewhere in the northern part of South Vietnam. Ironically, that particular day, the newspapers reported that a naval hospital under construction in South Vietnam had been overrun and destroyed by the enemy. My friend wondered whether that was my destination and quipped about what I intended to do when I got over there, assuming the hospital was now a pile of rubble.

The next day I took a commercial plane to San Francisco, which is quite close to Travis Air Force Base and my ultimate departure point from the United States. Indeed, the fear I had experienced leaving St. Louis was no longer in evidence. It had returned and disappeared several times, and then it entirely evaporated as I spent more time training at Camp Pendleton. My perception was that I was emotionally buoyed up by the military associates I met and interacted with at the base. Presumably I was truly gaining a sense of personal, though not professional, security about the next year of my life.

I contacted another neurosurgeon, who I trained with at the Mayo Clinic, and his wife. Although they were surprised to see that I was in the navy and on my way to Vietnam, they did not seem to harbor that same ostensible fear that the woman on the airliner from St. Louis had been gripped with. We visited and had lunch at their home, after which we said good-bye.

Since I still had a little time, I wandered about San Francisco. I took a taxicab to the Mark Hopkins Hotel, which at that time was one of the highest buildings in San Francisco, and rode the elevator to the top of the hotel, where there was a restaurant and impressive panoramic view of the city of San Francisco and San Francisco Bay. It was late in the afternoon as I sat at the bar, looking out over the Golden Gate Bridge and San Francisco Bay, watching ships and small boats moving about. After a few drinks, that familiar fear came back. I wondered if I might get killed. I wondered if I'd made the biggest mistake of my life thus far, but I managed to shake off this paranoia. I told myself that it was natural to be worried. In fact, it would have been quite unnatural to not be worried and fearful.

My next step to departure was a stop at the Treasure Island Naval Base, which is in the center of San Francisco Bay. That was where I'd get transportation to Travis Air Force Base about thirty miles inland. That's what I did. I was directed to a large civilian contract bus. There were about thirty other individuals on board from different branches of the military. After twenty or thirty minutes, we left Treasure Island and headed across the Oakland Bay Bridge to Travis.

Travis Air Force Base functions as one of the major military air transportation facilities for the air force. At that time, it operated large aircraft that were about the size of a Boeing 707 and were called C-141s, built by Lockheed.

These planes looked somewhat different from the civilian 707s in that the wings were mounted high on the fuselage and draped down as they radiated laterally to the tips on either side, much like the wings of a gull in flight. The planes were painted a dark-olive drab and, of course, included the identification markers of the US Air Force.

After alighting from the bus at the air terminal at Travis, I presented my orders to air force personnel on the other side of the passenger desk. Following review of the orders, they advised me that the next plane to Saigon would be departing the next afternoon. I then went over to the officers' BOQ and arranged for lodging.

The plane was delayed for various reasons, but it eventually took off, and I was on my way to Vietnam. Since the plane was essentially a freight carrier, it had no windows, but in my mind's eye I pictured leaving the coast behind and moving out over the broad blue Pacific. I wondered if I'd seen the last of my country forever, and I am sure some of the other 150 or so men on the plane with me were thinking the same thing.

No one spoke. I doubt anyone was acquainted, although all were going to the same place, a war. We were told there was coffee in back by an impersonal air force male attendant. Internal appointments were nonexistent. The outside of the plane was a dark, dull green, while the inside was a bit lighter but uniformly green. Cabin lighting was dim and emanated from recessed fixtures in the roof. There were no windows.

This was hardly a cheerful environment: monotony dominated, uniform dark-colored interior, dim lighting, immobile robot-like passengers staring into space, unchallenged drone of the engines, musty odor, and "sergeant personality," the flight attendant who did not give a damn. My unwelcome companion, "shroud of fear," again encased me, and sat beside me for at least two hours.

After about three hours in the air, we were each provided with a small white cardboard box in which were a sandwich, potato chips, and some cookies. I wandered back from my seat to obtain coffee, not so much because I liked it, but rather as a distraction from the monotonously droning engines and the sight of the dimly lit, windowless cabin of the airplane. The coffee container was a large metal cylinder with a spigot at the bottom. It was strapped to a shelf in the back of the plane. The hours seemed to drone like the engines, on and on. In all, it would take eighteen hours to get to Vietnam.

I found myself thinking too much about my lack of experience as a neurosurgeon. I wondered if I was man enough and doctor enough to meet the challenges that were just over the horizon. I was fully aware that within a few days I would probably be dealing with major brain injuries, and although I had gained some sense of confidence as a neurosurgeon while in my brief stint in Milwaukee, I was far from technically adept, and now I would be much more distant from either the actual assistance or consultative recommendations of another neurosurgeon. Patients might well live or die on the basis of my primarily vicarious experience rather than my actual capability.

Additionally, the rather elaborate surgical operating suite I had to work in in Milwaukee and that available in the Mayo Clinic were far from a possibility and only a memory where I was going. The notion crept into my mind that I had no right to be masquerading as a neurosurgeon and taking on the enormity of the responsibility in a combat field hospital setting. Whatever the facts (or myriad of them) were that propelled me to this point were now plunging me directly into probably the most difficult technical challenge of my life now or in the future. The play was set in motion, and there was no turning back.

Most of the passengers tried to sleep during the long flight, though I suspect, like mine, it was a fitful sleep replete with frequent nightmares and anticipated expectations of what was to befall us some 12,000 miles away. Several men on this plane were not coming back! After approximately eight hours of flying, the aircraft commander advised us that we would be landing on Wake Island for refueling and about a two-hour break.

We deplaned and were allowed to wander about. It was in the middle of the night. As I walked down the stairwell to the ground, the very pleasant sound and sensation of a South Sea breeze from the nearby ocean gently brushed across my face. In the rather near distance I could hear the ocean surf. Looking in the distance, I could see where the stars met the ocean just a short distance away. Astronomy was my hobby. We must have gone a long way south because the constellations in the sky were unfamiliar. The island was quite small; indeed from the runway you could see the surf on one side of the island less than five hundred yards away. The moon was bright, lighting up the surroundings in a soothing silvery glow.

I believe it was about 1:00 a.m. The pale moon glow splashed across several palm trees that bent gently in the South Sea breeze. Since there was ample time, I wandered over toward the beach and looked out over the South Pacific. As the waves rolled in, the crests of each seemed to reflect a silvery iridescence, the illusion of a lighted road leading from the ocean to the beach. The soft sandy beach, balmy temperature, and gentle breeze now clearly heard as it stroked its invisible fingers between the leaves of the palm trees were genuinely therapeutic for my intensifying anxiety. I knew where I was headed, yet this was stunningly mesmerizing.

I wandered along the beach with the ocean to my left and palm trees on the right. I mused back in time about twenty-four years (I was then a child) to the beginning of the Second World War, when Washington decided Wake Island could not be defended by the US forces in the early war time frame and was therefore simply written off to invasion and takeover by the Japanese.

It was defended by marines and quite possibly fathers of men I was going to be with for the next year. It was held for several days against overwhelming Japanese naval forces until it was overrun.

I wondered how many collections of bones from defending forces, and even enemy invading troops, were now embedded under the surface of this island and possibly under the strip of beach beneath my feet. I also wondered how ironic it was that in less than a quarter of a century, the United States found itself immersed in another war deep in the South Pacific.

Returning to reality, I walked back to the airstrip and into the air terminal, where we were soon notified that the plane was refueled and passengers would be instructed to load shortly. After a brief time, we did just that. The single door behind the cockpit on the left side again closed, and the sensation that I was in a long narrow sarcophagus again erupted. I settled back in my seat, the engines again were brought up sequentially to taxi power, and we began to roll. Within ten minutes we had come to a stop. The plane again turned into position on the active runway, and as the engines accelerated to takeoff power, the plane again started to creep. Then it accelerated and again rotated, and one could feel, though not see, us lift off the ground. Even if there had been windows, we could see nothing less the moon and inky darkness.

I was now very tired and fell asleep for the next few hours. I awoke with the heavy sluggish feeling one gets from inadequate fitful sleep. I looked at my watch, which indicated that it had been nearly seventeen hours since we left Travis Air Force Base. The engines droned on, and the tedium stretched away to infinity. I walked to the left at end of the airplane for coffee and used the opportunity to stretch somewhat and reorient myself.

After a few more hours, the aircraft commander notified us from the flight deck that we were approaching Saigon and would be landing within thirty minutes. The ugly "demon of fear," which had been suppressed by my fatigue and my pleasant distraction on Wake Island, awakened and reared its head.

As the plane began to descend, my imagination switched into nervous overdrive. I entertained the thought that the airport would be relatively modern with a moderate-sized air terminal and congested with airliners from exotic parts of the world. I then reasoned, however, that this was ridiculous. Saigon is a war-torn country, and not only would commercial airliners not be landing at this field for safety reasons, but even if they were allowed to, what manner of tourists would come to war-racked South Vietnam? I then speculated that the field would be of a military style with unimposing buildings surrounding the runways and multiple military aircraft standing about in various stages of preparation, with equipment-loading personnel moving about in a methodical fashion.

In the midst of my musing, the plane touched ground, gradually rolled to a stop, turned and moved a short distance again, and came to another stop, whereupon the engines shut down and the front door was opened.

5

ALIEN WORLD

I WALKED DOWN THE STAIRWELL AND toward the blast furnace of Tan-Son-Nhut, the name of the airfield serving the beleaguered city of Saigon. I looked about and on the periphery of the runway saw relatively small one- and two-story dirty stucco buildings with flat roofs surrounded by scattered vegetation and absolutely no landscaping. Barbed wire rolls surrounded the field. Troops and rifles were everywhere. Anti-aircraft batteries were scattered about.

I was directed toward the other end of the runway, a huge weed-covered unimproved field on which a large array of various military short-range aircraft were distributed. I saw no warplanes, the kind that carried weapons, just lots of helicopters and single-engine prop planes that were probably used for observation. In another area were larger two-engine, high-wing, boxlike fuselage planes with a rear door arranged like a drawbridge. These craft, I subsequently learned, were called C-123 cargo planes.

A group of us from the air force transport plane were simply advised to walk onto the grass field with the numerous military aircraft and ask which one was going toward each of our ultimate destinations. My orders indicated I was to proceed to Da Nang. I was carrying my single military cloth suitcase (seabag). As required, I was wearing my tan travel uniform that included a tie and an overlying khaki blouse with rank-identifying shoulder boards and a typical navy beaked hat referred to as a "cover." The heat was oppressive. I wandered through the beaten-down straw grass field from aircraft to aircraft. I noted the planes to be in various stages of servicing by crewmen. These men were generally stripped to the waist while working on engines or other parts of the airplane.

I felt like a hitchhiker. I asked crew members near various planes how to get to Da Nang. Generally they had no idea. I finally made my way to one of the two-engine C-123s and observed that one crewman had the cowling off of the starboard engine and was sitting up on the wing, straddled over the engine, looking like a mounted horseman while carrying out some sort of maintenance on the thing.

Meanwhile the pilot and copilot were leaning up against the shaded side of the plane, smoking cigarettes. They were dressed in the camouflage uniforms so typical of the area and had their covers cocked back on their heads, looking rather nonchalant. One of them wore a sidearm on his right hip, while the other had the same and also had a bandolier of ammunition slung over his shoulder, angling down off his right hip. I must have looked peculiar, dressed in a stateside, seemingly formal uniform. Indeed, I was so tired, frustrated, and scared, I cared not what they thought!

I inquired as to how to get to Da Nang, whereupon they indicated that the type of airplane they flew is a combined freight and passenger plane that moves between the various military enclaves throughout Vietnam on a routine basis during daylight hours for resupply and troop transport.

They further advised that you can look at the nose of the plane and tell by its painted configurations where it will eventually end up. They went on to say that the type of plane I wanted was a C-123 that had a white-and-gray checkerboard configuration on its nose cone.

I again picked up my seabag, now more tired than scared or frustrated. I turned and looked around in a detached fashion, searching the enormous field for a twin-engine airplane with a white-and-gray checkerboard nose. After about a half hour of roaming from aircraft to aircraft, I spotted my prey and descended upon it like a hungry eagle. It too was undergoing some sort of maintenance of one of the engines. The engine cowling was laying on the ground beneath the wing. A grease-covered crewman was standing beneath the engine, wrench in hand, while standing on the top of an ammunition case. Again the pilot and copilot dressed in fatigues were standing nearby, either discussing international politics, Aristotelian logic, or, more likely, their girlfriends.

They were standing under the shade of one wing and were in various states of disarray, unshaven, sweaty uniforms, covers either tipped backward or off to the right, noticeably bearing sidearms with an extra cache of ammunition in a clip on the opposite hip. I identified myself, was saluted, returned the salute, and inquired as to whether or not I could go with them to Da Nang. They indicated, "By all means," specifying they would be there before nightfall although there would be a few stops on the way. They suggested that I throw my baggage inside.

This type of plane had a cargo door in the back that resembled a bridge across a moat in the days of feudal castles, such that it could be lowered to the ground for passage and then raised upward for flight, in the familiar drawbridge mode.

The cargo door was angled down against the ground, inclined at about thirty degrees. I struggled with my seabag and then walked up the ramp into the cargo compartment, which was about seven feet high, six to seven feet wide, and fifteen feet long. It was half-full of boxes, stamped with identification, including food, mail, and ammunition. Since there were no other passengers about, I assumed I would be their only human cargo. After securing my bag to the deck of the cargo compartment with a canvas strap, I went outside again and conversed with the pilots. They stated that the day before, a C-123 on takeoff had been shot down and was still laying shattered in multiple jagged parts beyond the distant end of the runway and that it would be visible as we took off. This comment did little to settle the anxiety now replaced by outright fear. I felt a desperate need to engage in any form of self-preservation.

Within about an hour, the crewman who was working on the engine completed his task, assembled the cowling about the engine, and declared the plane airworthy. The pilots told me to climb in the cargo compartment, strap myself in, and enjoy the ride. They cautioned me that takeoffs would be steep and that descents into the various outlying fields where they had to deposit their supplies would also be quite steep since snipers frequently waited for approaching aircraft and attempted to shoot them down as they descended or departed from the airstrips.

The pilots climbed into their positions in the forward compartment, and the crew chief/engine mechanic got in the back with me and pulled a lever on the bulkhead of the compartment, and I watched as the long, flat loading door slowly lifted up and closed off the back of the compartment to the outside. Although the comfort index of the large plane from which I just departed was nothing to behold, this craft was a quantum step below that. Indeed, I was sitting on an ammunition case that was up against the bulkhead to which I secured my canvas safety belt. I was bathed in a swirling heat.

First the starboard or right engine began to groan as its starter turned the crankshaft. It seemed to cough several times and then roared into life with an enormous noise, not the least bit muffled from the cargo compartment. Smoke from the exhaust billowed into the cargo compartment. The entire plane vibrated as it was brought up to power. I could barely hear the port-side engine start; however, I felt the vibration of the plane increase dramatically.

After a minute or two, we began to roll over the weed-covered field and back toward the tarmac of the main runway, whereupon we came to a halt and waited several minutes before again taxiing farther onto the active runway. The few portholes along the bulkheads were uncovered. Even without glass in these side portholes, the wash from the propellers was stifling heat. The plane turned slowly into proper position and shuddered as the two engines were advanced up to full power while the brakes were held. Moments later, the brakes were released and we began to move slowly and then ever more rapidly down the runway, vibrating forcefully and shuddering slightly as we slowly lifted into the sky. The intense noise of the engines, the absence of window glass, and the banging cases of cargo were muffled slightly by my intense fatigue. I didn't notice until we were airborne that one could look down through the floor of the cargo compartment and see trees and terrain passing below us through scattered holes in the bottom of the plane. The plane banked to the left about a mile or two beyond the end of the runway so that the pilots could get a better look at the plane that had crashed the day before. I looked down and viewed the distorted corpse of a partly burned C-123 cargo plane.

Although I had been gripped by fear when I left St. Louis, again when I was in the bar in San Francisco, and when I boarded the military transport jet at Travis, I was resolute in going to Vietnam. At this moment, however, I felt more than ever that I had made a mistake by volunteering for this endeavor. Clearly I was a coward and did not belong here. Looking about the cargo compartment I noticed the various containers and boxes, ammunition, food, rifles, body bags, and mail. The scene of those bags hammered firmly in my psyche the reason the navy was so eager to send me here. It made me shiver even in this heat.

I also studied the aluminum rib structures along the bulkheads on either side and along the roof of the cabin. Then finally I stared directly at the crew chief, sitting in the cargo compartment across the compartment from me. He was sitting on a box stenciled "grenades." His eyes were directed out one of the side ports, staring dispassionately into space. He was dressed in a dirty, wrinkled, greasy-looking, camouflage-colored field uniform like everyone else. He wore heavy black boots and also a gun belt strapped around his waist with a weapon in its holster, hanging off his right hip with additional ammunition slung from the gun belt over his left hip.

His look was one of total nonchalance and complacence, completely devoid of fear. His bored demeanor conveyed a sense of confidence, suggesting that he had ridden this plane a thousand times in every conceivable risk scenario and continues to survive. My anxiety, born of fear, was so minimized by his ostensible attitude that I settled back a bit as the plane, hot as it was even at reasonable altitude, bumped and rumbled along toward what was referred to as the highlands of the South Vietnam countryside. *Those holes in the bottom of this plane—what was their origin?*

In my mind there was a blurring of the distinction between two things: fear and fatigue.

After flying for about forty minutes, the plane abruptly angled downward at a steep angle of descent just as I had been pre-advised. I hoped the snipers were asleep, having lunch, or dreaming of their girlfriends. After the rapid descent, the plane leveled off again just as abruptly as it had begun and seemed to touch the runway almost immediately. It, like many airliners, was capable of reversing its propellers and shortening its landing roll. I believe we came to a stop within less than a hundred yards.

Again the drawbridge-like cargo door was lowered, and I looked out across the runway that was nothing more than a dirt strip carved by some sort of heavy equipment from the jungle. Indeed the trees literally surrounded the strip as close as sixty yards from any margin. This was Da Lat. Scattered tents occupied by the special forces units assigned there were seen along the side of the runway, and special forces members were seen here and there, carrying automatic weapons or rifles moving like robots oblivious to the threat.

Two or three of them came up to the plane, climbed into the cargo compartment, and off-loaded several of the boxes. I stood beside the craft with the pilots as one of the special forces officers told us that the night before there had been heavy Viet Cong activity in the area. He commented that the VC had waited until dark, then in twos and threes crawled through thick grass to the edge of the runway with rifles. They were silent, and had it not been for the frequent use of flashlights by the security members, an ambush could have ensued. The light reflected from a rifle, however, triggered a burst of machine gunfire by the special forces, sending at least ten figures diving into the thick brush.

We stayed less than fifteen minutes and then taxied

quickly into takeoff position, raising large dust clouds from the propeller blast, and the engines surged to full power with brakes gripping. The pilot then released them and raced down the runway, angled very sharply upward, and climbed into the sky. If they were waiting for us, they missed. After two more similar stops we headed for Da Nang.

It took about an hour and a half to make the flight, and it was uneventful.

The jungle terrain below us was a deep brilliant green and, indeed, a beautiful sight. As we drifted down along the flatlands, rice paddies began to come into evidence as geometric shades of light green. They too were beautiful.

The plane began to descend in a more normal fashion toward the Da Nang area and touched uneventfully down on the runway. We taxied for a while and then came to a stop. The pilots advised me that they would stay in Da Nang overnight, saluted, and wished me good luck. Then with the crew chief, they headed toward their squadron Quonset hut.

I picked up my bag, got out of the plane, and stepped on a relatively well-developed long tarmac runway. On the sides of the runway I could see various buildings, all Quonset huts—olive drab, unimpressive in their style, uniform in their appearance, and typically military. The runway and the buildings were surrounded by thick concertina wire (barbed wire), and there were guards carrying rifles at intervals along the fence line in addition to which were sandbagged more secure guard positions segmented at strategic intervals just inside the concertina wire and surrounding the entire airfield.

Off toward one end I could see several tactical aircraft, F-4 Phantom jets, olive drab with USAF stencils just behind the wings on the fuselage. I noticed that the planes were being kept in what appeared to be aluminum cubicles ten feet or so high so that a partition of aluminum separated one plane from the adjacent plane, with another wall of this aluminum-like structure behind the plane and up against the concertina wire. Each looked like a one-car garage without a roof. I was unsure of the logic; however, I did suspect that this was designed to prevent any incoming mortar or artillery round from damaging more than one plane at a time.

The sun was sinking into the evening sky toward the highland region. The sky was a deepening blue, and shadows were forming, ominous, dark, and unwelcoming. It was evident that it would be dark in an hour, and I would be swallowed by the night. With troops moving here and there, I felt like an orphan, confused and afraid. I was a doctor who was sent here to do surgery. Where were my assistants? Where was my driver? Who even cared? *What the hell am I doing here?*

I walked up to a marine who was standing by a jeep and asked him if he would take me to the G-4 hospital. (My orders specified such.) He looked at me somewhat quizzically and indicated that it would not be wise at this late hour since it was several miles from the airstrip over unsecured roadway, and furthermore the hospital had been attacked and essentially destroyed within the last several days and thus no longer operative. I realized at this point that the newspaper report that I had read in San Diego preceding the trip referred indeed to this hospital. The place I gave up my freedom and comfort for and then traveled halfway around the globe to do neurosurgery for—it no longer existed!

I now truly was abandoned, useless, and lost. I had come 12,000 miles to the ashes of my objective. What a mistake! I asked the marine with the jeep if he had any idea what I could do, at least for that night. He indicated that there was a facility in the center of Da Nang that was the headquarters for naval operations relating to marine activities in and around the Da Nang area. He said that he could take me there and quite possibly they could help provide for an alternate assignment. We got in the jeep with my bag and drove from the air base a distance of about two miles into the city of Da Nang, which itself was a series of old one- and two-story, flat-roof stucco-walled French buildings with dirty, unpaved streets and scattered puddles of water along the side of the roads. There were no streetlights. I found out later that sewage from the homes dumped in the street was the source of the foul odor one perceived as we drove through the town on the way to the naval support headquarters.

The headquarters was in a somewhat larger old French building surrounded by concertina wire and marine guards. The driver took me to the entrance, where a sentry looked at my orders, saluted, and instructed me to pass through the gate. I returned the salute, bid the marine driver good-bye, and after expressing my gratitude, saluted him, took my seabag from his jeep, and walked into the headquarters with my now dirty, sweaty, and grease-smeared stateside navy uniform. Not only was I dismayed, frightened, and tired but now I was embarrassed. Once inside, I presented my orders to the "officer of the day" sitting behind an old desk with a small gooseneck lamp, working over a series of documents. There was a small electric fan on one corner of his desk. He greeted me warmly and advised me that they were fully aware that there would be several incoming physician personnel for the now-destroyed G-4 hospital.

I was provided with C rations and a bed (sort of). Since I had not had adequate sleep for nearly thirty-six hours, I fell into a deep combination of sleep and coma. I did not awaken until the following morning. I got up, washed as best as I could from a bucket of water provided for me, shaved and brushed my teeth with the same water, put on my less-than-acceptable uniform, and walked from my sleeping quarters to the front of the headquarters building, where I met a navy hospital administrative officer.

"We're cutting you orders for duty at Charlie Med," he said.

I wondered what Charlie Med was, but I didn't ask.

"You'll stay there until the G-4 hospital is rebuilt, and then you'll transfer there," he continued.

I nodded.

"What exactly is Charlie Med, sir?" I finally asked.

He explained that it was one of three marine hospitals under marine control in that sector of Vietnam. "It's C Medical Company, Third Force Service Support Group, Third Marine Division. Able and Bravo Medical Companies are located sixty miles north and thirty miles south of Da Nang," he said.

He went on to say that these field hospitals were supposed to be mobile, like MASH units in Korea. "They got to be able to bug out in two days or less," he said.

"Guess they're close to the action," I said, trying not to sound too nervous.

"Sure are!" he said. "Right smack-dab in the thick of all the fun!"

"Oh," I said.

I was then provided with a handgun, a gun belt, and ammunition. I was instructed to wear it at all times.

"Good luck," the officer said.

I saluted, suspecting I was going to need all the luck I could get.

CHARLIE MED

My marine driver sped out of Da Nang in a mud-spattered jeep, and soon we were roaring past lush rice paddies and into increasingly thick jungle. It was late October, and yet the heat was incredible, totally alien to what I was used to in the Midwest. Back home the leaves would be turning color, but not here. Sweat poured off me in spite of the breeze in the open vehicle as it bumped and thumped over a muddy trail deeper and deeper into the bush. I reflected briefly on how much my life had changed since January, a time when I had nothing more to worry about than starting a private practice. Some years are momentous in a man's life, and 1965 was certainly that for me.

We covered the roughly ten miles to Charlie Med as rapidly as the driver could go, and I wondered if he was worried about snipers or if he was scared about driving on the road at night and just wanted to get back to the city. My first impression of Charlie Med as we rolled in bordered on shock. I had known conditions would be primitive, and that's what they were.

The field hospital sat in a clearing several hundred yards outside of thick surrounding jungle. It was defined by a series of khaki-colored "hard back tents" that varied in size, adjacent to which was a helicopter-landing platform with a large red cross. Surrounding the entire area at a distance of about seventy yards was a perimeter of concertina wire. Just inside the barbed wire perimeter were foxholes spaced about seventy to eighty yards apart, each manned by one or two marines armed with an M-16 rifle. I soon found out that marines shot off rifle flares at night to light up the area, hoping to discourage the Viet Cong from paying a visit.

My driver said good-bye and hightailed it back to Da Nang, leaving me staring at what would be my home for the foreseeable future. I asked to see the chief of surgery, and I was directed to Commander Greg Grew. He was surprised to see a neurosurgeon for two reasons: he was not expecting one, and there were no surgical instruments available to do neurosurgery.

I asked Commander Grew why that was. He explained that nobody had informed him of my arrival, and so no preparations had been made. The confusion resulted from the fact that my duty station, the naval hospital, had been destroyed and that I'd been found another assignment on the fly.

Commander Grew dutifully took me on a tour of the hospital, but I suspected he thought I was an imposter. During the course of the tour, he inquired how long I had trained. I assumed he was referring to the brief course in "field medicine" at Camp Pendleton, and I responded, "Two weeks."

"I recognize that's long enough to learn neurosurgery," he said, starting to smile, "but how long were you at the university?"

Realizing the misunderstanding, I explained, and we both began to laugh.

As we continued our tour, I focused on the assemblage of tents that comprised the core of Charlie Med. These included a large tent with a plywood floor adjacent to the helicopter landing zone that was used as a shock tent. This shock tent, as it was referred to, was the first line of medical management after the patient was removed from the helicopter. This particular tent was about thirty-five by fifteen feet. Each end of this tent was open to the elements, with one end facing the tarmac from which the patients arrived and the other end representing an exit through which patients, after emergency management was rendered, were transferred to either surgery or the intensive care unit, which itself was an even larger tent.

Within twenty yards of the shock tent was situated a small X-ray tent in which a military field X-ray unit was located. Nearby was another medium-sized tent surrounded by sandbags built up around each of the four sides of the structure to a height of approximately six feet. I was told this provided some protection from incoming mortar rounds.

Inside this tent were two cramped operating rooms separated by a canvas wall-like curtain. The floor was plywood, thus affording some semblance of cleanliness. A single overhead light hung in the center of each of the operating rooms, below which was a primitive-appearing operating table.

Anesthesia machines of the field unit variety were at the head of each operating table. The entrance to the operating room tent was via a single canvas flap, so to speak, doorway. This was the only tent on the base that had air-conditioning ducted in through a six- to ten-inch flexible conduit from a motor-driven air-conditioning unit standing beside the tent. It would be an understatement to use the term *austere* to describe this operating room in which I was to work.

Within thirty yards of the operating room was another fairly large tent with a plywood floor, and several small lights hanging from the vaulted ceiling of the tent. In this structure were approximately forty cots used for postoperative patient management.

At one end of this tent were a small desk and a box on which a corpsman could sit for purposes of chart management. It also represented a vantage point from which he could observe each of the patients. Intravenous fluid in one-liter storage bottles was used for infusion purposes in the postoperative patients. These bottles were connected to a typical intravenous tubing on the distal end of which was a needle that could be inserted into a patient's arm vein and through which fluid could be dripped at a variable rate into the victim while he lay in his rack. The bottles themselves were slung from a long cable strung from one end of the tent to the other and positioned directly over the heads of the row of cots. This, like most other tents, had one single opening through a canvas-covered doorway or flap. Crude light fixtures also were slung from the A-frame–like tent roof and were supported at a level about seven feet above the plywood floor. They provided reasonable lighting for the corpsmen to discharge their duties.

At a slightly greater distance from this acute patient-management area were tents of various sizes for administrative purposes—one for a surgeons' conference room, and another much larger one of an elongated variety with an open walk-in area on one end, and an open area in the opposite end was used as the mess hall. It was arranged with a long buffet-like serving table made of crude unpainted pine boards laying across sawhorses. This buffet serving table stretched from one end of the tent to the other. This was the field kitchen from which the hospital personnel were provided most of their meals. Surgeons were also given cases of C rations in the event that they were tied up, dealing with patients during the food-serving hours. These cases were kept in our living tents. At the far end of the tent mess hall and just outside the open exit was a series of three forty-gallon galvanized trash cans, each filled with water heated by a military version of an immersion burner.

After an individual had passed along the serving line, the men would either go to mess tables on one side of the tent or simply walk outside and sit on the grass or lean against a tree while eating their dinner.

After the men had eaten their dinner, they walked to the far end of the mess tent and dipped their tray, supported by something that looked like an unraveled coat hanger, into each of the large cans of water in a sequential fashion. There was a brush in the first can so that you could wipe off foodstuff in the water. The second and third cans were used for simply jostling one's mess tray up and down and cleansing it this way in the rather hot water. Each of the men was then responsible for his own tray and routinely carried it back to his sleeping tent.

The remaining tents on the compound were used for housing officers and enlisted personnel, of which there were probably 120 (mostly corpsmen). These tents were dark, dismal, olive drab, and with a single lightbulb slung from a pole in the center. The floor of the tent was a raised plywood deck, while the sides of the tent were open save for mosquito netting. Each end of the tent was canvas covered except for the entrance, consisting of a flap cover, as were all the others. Notable here, like in each of the other tents on the compound, was a stale mildew odor that never cleared and permeated everything inside—including all clothing, I was soon to find out. Bunks were standard cots, with a sleeping bag on top and mosquito netting draped over each bunk.

At the entrance of the tent was a foxhole dug by the occupants in event of enemy attack and overrun. In the rainy season, Commander Grew warned me, these foxholes were always filled with water. The ground adjacent to the various tents was primarily of semisoft soil that was covered with mud puddles in the winter. He said about ten hospital administrators and forty to fifty corpsmen and security force marines completed the human complement. Protection was provided by marines in foxholes surrounding the tent hospital. They were about fifty feet outside the tents and situated at seventy to eighty-foot intervals and manned twenty-four hours a day.

All of this was a lot to take in, what with my having just arrived at Charlie Med, but I observed attentively and listened to everything Commander Grew said. We stopped in the center of the facility for a moment, and the commander talked more about the mud in such generous quantity everywhere.

"In late July, the Sea Bees were building this place," Grew said, "and they actually sunk a bulldozer right over there!"

"Sunk a bulldozer?" I asked, not knowing what to think.

"Yeah. Sunk it. The thing got stuck in the mud and literally sank." Grew pointed toward the center of the compound. "See that?"

"What?"

"That!"

I looked hard, but I didn't see a bulldozer anywhere. Then I noticed the end of what looked like a rusty pipe sticking up. "You mean that? What is that?" I asked.

"Exhaust pipe," Grew said, shaking his head. "It's a different world around here, I can tell you that!"

I guessed it was.

I then was assigned a tent, was assisted by a corpsman in placing my travel bag, including all of my belongings, and prepared to take call.

It was not until over a year later when both Commander Grew and I were reassigned to the naval hospital in San Diego and had become friends that he shared with me his suspicion that I was an impostor simply looking for an opportunity to practice on human beings. He told me a copy of my orders finally reached him about two to three weeks after I went to work for him. Such greatly ameliorated his anxiety.

He returned to the business at hand, namely orienting me to Charlie Med. He noted that this marine medical facility was designed for the single purpose of receiving battle injuries directly from the strike zone via rescue helicopters. Then after providing emergency and lifesaving surgical procedures, our mission was to transfer the patients by helicopter back to the Da Nang airstrip, where an air force hospital plane would be waiting to ferry the casualties to the air force military hospital in the Philippines about a thousand miles away. This flight was about five hours. Propeller evacuation planes, slower than jets, were used.

The situation was now clear in my mind. The challenge was enormous, and I was terrified. I knew my limits; the war did not!

I began taking calls as a neurosurgeon at Charlie Med within four hours after arriving at the compound. The sense of fear and intimidation I experienced was partly prompted by the austere and primitive nature of this medical and surgical environment, compared to what I had been accustomed to in my training as a neurosurgeon at the Mayo Clinic.

Indeed, the knowledge that the nearest neurosurgeon

to whom I might turn for advice was at least two hundred miles away at another military medical facility afforded little comfort to me. In fact, it scared the hell out of me! From a practical perspective, he may as well have been 10,000 miles away since contact by telephone or radio was out of the question. A major factor triggering my anxiety was the surgical equipment (or, I should say, lack of) available to me. It clearly was antiquated and not designed for neurosurgical operations. In fact, some of the assigned equipment was not even in the instrument container with which I was provided. Who knows where it had gone in the 12,000-mile trip from the United States to Da Nang? Maybe it was never placed in the container back in the States!

Unlike a civilian hospital where a trauma call would include one, two, or three injured individuals at one time, in this combat environment there might be a lull of many hours, following which two, three, or four helicopters would bring in a group of fifteen to eighteen injured marines from a firefight out in the jungle. You can't imagine the chaos when that happened. It still makes me dizzy to think about what we surgeons went through on heavy shifts, but what could we do other than our duty for those young men? No matter how hard it got, we mustered the courage to hold the line, just like they did. They faced fire, but we did too in our frequent futile efforts to save as many as we could.

Since the facility had only two very primitive operating rooms, there was the necessity of prioritization of injury cases. The chief of surgery, who also was the senior surgeon (no longer operating), would make a determination as to which patient had priority for each of the two operating rooms. The criteria were based on potential for the patient's survival and the length of the operative procedure. All neurosurgical procedures take an extended period of time, and the potential for survival is generally less than for individuals who have sustained injuries to the chest, abdomen, or limbs. It was woe to the guy who got his brains shot up versus the guy who got shot in the abdomen. The latter would get treated faster. Because of the Darwinism of triage, I was at the bottom of the list when it came to using one of the two operating rooms.

I worried about that right from the start, and it soon became obvious that I had good reason for concern.

7

TOIL AND TROUBLE

THE SUBSEQUENT DAYS AND WEEKS CONTINUED with periods of quiet followed by a deluge of battered and broken bodies. Some were alive and others dead. All were brought in by the now-familiar olive-drab–attired navy corpsmen manning their stretchers and carrying the victims from the side of the aircraft directly to the open shock tent twenty-five yards away. After disgorging itself of between three and five injured troops, the chopper, its engines still churning, would rev up and quickly lift off the tarmac to make room for a second similar craft, and then often a third and possibly a fourth, carrying a result of man's savagery to man.

Not uncommonly between 5 percent and 10 percent of the injured would be dead on arrival and, after confirmation by a medical examiner, would be carried across the tarmac to another group of tents known as the zone of Decedent Affairs. Here the bodies would be placed in black canvas-like bags. These were somewhat similar to a sleeping bag, including a zipper running the length of the bag and into which the body could be placed. The zipper could then be closed over the corpse and identification confirmed by dog tags. They were placed on stacks like cordwood until available helicopters could ferry them perfunctorily back to Da Nang. There they were placed on an air force plane for transfer back to first Clark Air Force Base in the Philippines, on to Honolulu, and finally to the Continental United States for subsequent burials. Hundreds and hundreds of marines I saw returned to their families in this way. Indeed, every dead body spoke of a personal tragedy.

As the injured were carried into the shock tent, it was understood that the surgeons would make themselves immediately available to assess the nature and extent of injuries and the potential for survival of each casualty. In such fashion, surgery and other nonsurgical efforts (or both) were decided upon and carried out. Others were turned down for formal care because of the hopelessness of their injuries. They were simply given morphine and pushed aside. Doctors sometimes play God, and we did frequently that year. I never ventured such would be necessary in the course of my protected education; however, I wasn't protected any longer and I was beyond my education.

It quickly became apparent that I was in over my head from a technical standpoint. My fears about a lack of actual operating experience were justified. Mistakes happened. The war happened. I probably killed some kids back in those early days at Charlie Med, killed them through my efforts to save their lives. That's an irony I was well aware of then, and it is one I am well aware of now. So was I a killer angel? Or was I just a kid like the rest of them who was simply trying to do his job? Okay, so I was at least ten years older than most of the guys who were over there at the time, but, in reality, I really was a kid just trying to find myself. When I think about it now, I like to think I saved more marines than I lost. I like to think that my abilities gave life more than my ineptitude took life. I like to think that, but I still can't forget what happened over there. I never will.

I recall one instance out of many where I found myself in trouble during surgery, with blasting artillery in the background, the moans and wails of the patients distracting and distressing me, the urgent orders from nearby doctors rising to a din, and the *thump,thump,thump* of still more choppers swooping in out of the bright blue sky with their burdens of blood, bone, and mangled bodies. The smells of the operating room remain with me, and sometimes the weirdest thing will bring them back again even now. I simply try not to think about it, and I almost always fail.

There is a long narrow blood channel just under the inner aspect of the skull that extends from the midpoint of the forehead to a bump on the back of the head. You can feel this with a finger, a midline prominence. At this location the channel divides into two branches, right and left, which then drain the blood to the jugular veins in the neck and then to the heart. This channel carries a rapidly flowing river of blood. Indeed, this channel carries 25 percent of the blood in the body.

With this bit of neuroanatomy and physiology background, the significance of this draining blood channel becomes more apparent. Partial or total interruption of blood inflow or outflow from the brain can lead very quickly to devastating consequences and probably death. Furthermore, this outflow tract I referred to is quite superficial on top of the brain, just barely under the skull and nearly fused to the rigid skull. Thus, an injury that might fracture or fragment the skull in this region on the top or back of the head could tear open this blood conveyance network and lead to enormous blood loss and possible exsanguination within minutes.

I had personal experience with this kind of injury one

night in the middle of surgery. I found myself on the one hand trying to control bleeding—by applying pressure with a sterile sponge to this torn or lacerated venous-draining network called the longitudinal sinus—so the patient did not bleed to death. However, when I would apply pressure, the blood circulating through the brain would be dramatically impaired, or damned up, and the brain would begin to swell from the pressure of the inflowing blood on the arterial side and impaired drainage on the venous end.

Knowing the man was in deep trouble, I desperately tried everything I could think of to help him. I found myself releasing my hand pressure against the torn longitudinal sinus to relieve the brain swelling, but then I was faced with the outflowing gush of massive amounts of wine-red blood. The blood flowed like it was being pumped from a water fountain. What I desperately needed was some way of reconnecting the torn edges of this venous blood drainage tract. In essence, I needed to fix the ruptured pipe. I will always remember the struggle. Blood sprayed and soaked everything—my hands, my sterile gown, the sterile drapes, and multiple cotton sponges that we'd put in to hold back the dam of blood in the patient's head. I had to relax the pressure, and that then allowed the brain swelling to subside, but, of course, I was greeted with another torrent of blood.

The scene was one of desperation and pure despair, a red cascade flowing from the head, radiating down the sterile drapes like a mountain stream, and then spreading like a pool of crimson tide, rising around the base of the operating table and staining my boots. At some point in each case the anesthesiologist would advise me that the patient's blood pressure had dropped to a subnormal level, and that the patient was dying. Despite every maneuver I knew, each young man with this type of injury uniformly left the operating room as a corpse. This remains one of the most devastating experiences of my life.

No sword or weapon of war could pierce a surgeon as deeply as the loss of a patient from an unsatisfactory operation. When I felt like I'd blown it, like I had let the man down and he died because of it, I folded up inside and hid in a dark place I still don't like to think about. Thankfully, those periods of depression were short-lived for the most part, though the memory of them is every bit as vivid as the real thing even all these years later. The physician-patient interactions were taken on with the intent of not only preserving life, but in restoring the soldier to a state of well-being so he could go out and kill more of the enemy. I gradually came to see that as a good cause, even when I failed miserably to actually carry out the mission on more than one sad occasion.

It is the nature of neurosurgery that successful operative results are considerably less frequent than those enjoyed by general surgeons, vascular surgeons, and eye surgeons. I knew that going in, even though I was still ignorant about most everything related to war in my first days at Charlie Med. Even the cardiac surgeons who routinely carried out complex operations on the heart had a higher patient survival and cure rate than surgeons in my field. I was fully aware of this when I entered neurosurgery as a young man, and to this day I am not embittered. It still doesn't make it any easier late at night, but I do accept it. I always have, come to think of it, even in those difficult days at Charlie Med in late 1965.

Back when I was an intern in 1960, I had a roommate who summed up what it's like to be a brain surgeon. The idea was that it is often a thankless and risky task. I remember him leaning back in his chair and saying, "Well, neurosurgeons don't win often, but when they do, they win big!"

Was he ever right, but he forgot to say we lose big too.

How many mothers, fathers, or young wives received devastating telegrams or visits to their homes from a navy chaplain, carrying the bad news? Had they any idea that the young man to whom they had said good-bye was now a rigid, grotesque piece of bloody matter plastered with human waste, mud, and quite possibly the blood of his pals, as well as his own? Would I for this nihilistic notion of the value of life meet a similar fate in the hereafter and be cast into Dante's Inferno? I thought about that a lot at Charlie Med, and it didn't do me much good.

One night I met Commander Grew on a muddy path near my tent. I could not sleep, so I had walked out in the dark to clear my head. The walk wasn't working very well, but I had to try. The nasty humid air practically suffocated me. The night was quiet, for once, which made it all the more eerie. Was Charlie out there? I knew the marine guards were, and I made sure not to spook them.

My commander stopped and took a good hard look at me. I looked back at him. The two of us just stood there for a long moment. He looked exhausted and upset. He was older than me and had much more experience in surgery and dealing with people. This man was fully aware of the impact a surgical case gone bad leaves on a surgeon. I don't remember exactly what he said to me, but to put it in somewhat rarified language, the man said, "Lieutenant, it's most frustrating to lose your grip on a patient while attempting to extract him from the jaws of death. However, young man, that's how it is out here! Keep in mind you are the only thing the troops have between them and a military cemetery!"

I thanked the commander, and we both parted ways, each lost in thought. As I walked slowly back to my tent, I remembered when I was a kid in World War II and I'd seen the small rectangular silk flag in our window, indicating that family members were in uniform defending our country. Similar flags were everywhere, practically one in every five houses. The flags were eight by twelve inches with an outer rectangular rim of blue. The small center was solid red, and imprinted on the red center was a white star indicating that one household member was committed to the war effort in a uniform. If more than one man had gone to war, an additional star was printed on the red background.

These flags were routinely hung in the front window, usually in the living room, for all to see. When I rode my bike through the local neighborhoods I saw the flags wherever I went. If a star on the flag was gold, it communicated to all that a family member had been killed in the war. I saw many gold-star homes in St. Louis during the course of the Second World War. Somehow, thinking about that made the tough emotions of the evening recede a little. I went back into my tent and tried to sleep.

The days at Charlie Med began to blur together. In the end, I wasn't there all that long, just a matter of a couple of months, but it seemed like an eternity. Thanksgiving came and went. I wrote letters home. That helped a little. Connecting with family always did. As the holidays approached, I wondered what my former partner was doing, how much money was streaming into the practice I'd given up. I wondered why I'd been stupid enough to sign on for the blood, guts, and gore of brain surgery at a forward marine field hospital. I wondered about a lot of things.

The daily grind of bodies began when the choppers flew in. Then the stretchers were placed across sawhorses, making it relatively uncomplicated to transfer a patient from the helicopter to a resuscitation position in the shock tent. The unpainted plywood floor was always spattered with a crimson stain of both wet and dried blood. I eventually got used to it. I eventually didn't even notice it.

The patients were lined in rows perpendicular to the length of the tent and on each side of the tent such that a center aisle was created that extended from one end of the shock tent to the other for efficient entrance and egress for both patients and attending personnel. Intravenous solutions were supported by a stout wire strung from each end of the tent and on each side of the tent such that the wire would run perpendicular to the length of the stretchers and at about eye level. In this fashion various IV solutions, including saline, plasma substitute, and blood, could be suspended above the casualty and infused as rapidly as possible. True, it was primitive, yet it was functional.

We the surgeons would quickly move about this tent and confirm the type of injury among the various casualties and would then institute treatment if emergency management was indicated. We then made on-the-spot recommendations with respect to surgery or conservative management. Again with only two operating rooms available, as noted, the highest priority was given to individuals who had the highest probability of survival and could be managed in the operating tent in the shortest period of time. This was by anyone's estimate rationed care. If this policy had not been rigidly adhered to in such a blunt fashion, the number of required body bags would have increased and many more numbed and broken families would be grieving back home.

I recall one individual lying on his back with blood about his face and head. His helmet was off, and he was clearly in shock. When I inspected his scalp, there was a rent from his right eyebrow upward, directly back, adjacent to the long axis (sagittal dimension) of the head. Through this, I could see a fracture of his skull appearing much like the large crevice of an earthquake fault that had ruptured. It too extended from his forehead to the back of his head. The separation in the crack measured approximately an inch. Deep to this was the torn cranial covering we call the Dura Mater, deep to which was the typical soft gelatinous mixture of blood and grayish milky-colored material that might be described as egg-white brain tissue. This was dripping from his head to the plywood floor, creating an ever-increasing diameter of crimson and gray liquid and gelatin. This man died as I evaluated him!

Many patients had multiple penetrating wounds that were due to exploding devices, such as hand grenades, land mines, and incoming mortar rounds. A classic explosive device planted by the enemy along jungle trails was called the Bouncing Betty. This thing, when triggered by the foot of a trooper moving through the woods, would bound upward via a loaded spring device to about the mid-abdomen or thigh level, and then explode so as to achieve maximum destructive force among personnel within fifteen to twenty feet. From my perspective, this was a very effective weapon. It was not uncommon to see a patient after his flak vest, helmet, cartridge belt and jungle uniform removed to see he was inflicted in five to twenty separate penetration sites, including his arms, legs, abdomen, chest, face, and, of course, head. In such situations it was necessary for the patient to go to surgery and to be ministered to simultaneously by a general surgeon, orthopedist, and neurosurgeon.

Sterility in these operating rooms was less than optimal, a dream. A typical operating room environment in the United States is such that the surgeon is able to change his clothes and put on a clean scrub gown in one room, following which he has time to wash his hands for many minutes in another area. Then he enters the operating theater, where he is assisted in putting on a sterile surgical gown that reaches from his neck to his knees and has long sleeves reaching down to his wrists. Over that he is assisted with sterile glove application. His face is covered with a mask, and his head is also covered with a clean surgical cap.

In our jungle facility, however, we did not enjoy this traditional luxury. Indeed, all surgery was done in full jungle dress while wearing a flak jacket and a cartridge belt supporting a .45-caliber personal weapon hanging from our waist. Although we had gowns to pull over this form of attire, they were not sterile. We did have gloves that were sterile for a period of time, and we did wear a face mask. All surgery was carried out with marginal lighting and antiquated equipment. Although cleanliness was attempted, sterility was a joke! The distant sound of the artillery fire and the frequent roar of helicopter engines were ever present while we carried out surgery at Charlie Med.

The Marine Corps was responsible for the military action in the northern one-quarter of the country of South Vietnam. As noted before, organic to the marines are field hospitals staffed by navy physicians, of which Charlie Med was one. After information had been transmitted to the surgical chiefs of each of the other sections that a neurosurgeon was stationed at Charlie Med, all subsequent head injuries bypassed the other facilities and were brought directly via "Huey" to us.

Thus, with progression of time, an increased number of head injuries came under my domain and I found myself doing operations more and more commonly. Fortunately, some of the time I did have access to one or the other of the existing operating rooms at our facility, which represented a quantum leap higher than the picnic table that operating room was I referred to previously. Because I had an anesthesiologist, better lighting, better aspiration equipment, and more effective electrocautery equipment in these operating theaters, I was able to achieve a measure of enhanced results. Just as importantly, however, because of the frequency with which I was doing surgery, my surgical skills were improving at an incremental rate.

On occasions, the victims would have wounds of the chest, abdomen, and/or limbs in addition to the head, and as previously noted, I found myself doing cranial surgery while other surgeons were working on other parts of the body. This was another unpleasant revelation for me. Neurosurgery is delicate enough in a patient who does not move during the course of anesthesia. When, however, another surgeon is working on the abdomen and his assistant is pulling on the retractors or an orthopedist is working on a shattered arm, trying to manipulate it into a semi- anatomic position, the patients frequently are shifted about somewhat on the operating table. This, of course, translates to movement of the head, which in my case further degraded my technique and magnified my less-than-skillful surgical technique.

I seemed to alternate emotionally between insecurity and self-disdain during lulls in the surgical activity. One predawn night while in the midst of troubled sleep, I vacillated between the notion that I had misrepresented myself to the navy as a neurosurgeon when I was, in fact, looking for an escape from life, and a moment later I conjectured that I was simply incompetent. As the gray streaks of dawn peeked out on the horizon, I was terror-stricken with the reality that I must face another day of false representation as a neurosurgeon to several trusting marines. Anticipation of failure was my constant companion.

More than once I would have a delicate instrument inside the brain to pinch off and coagulate a small bleeding vessel, when suddenly the patient's head would jerk about, my instrument would be pulled from the brain, and the now-torn vessel would bleed more profusely, making it more difficult for me to proceed. After multiple frustrating attempts, usually I would be successful in securing a bleeding point, removing damaged brain tissue, reducing the pressure in the patient's head, which was one of my objectives, and closing the wound in at least a semi-acceptable fashion.

As time passed, it became an increasingly unpleasant way to learn and to gain skill. Men died. Yet, strangely enough, a sort of inner transformation was taking place within me. I could feel it. Every day when the artillery boomed, and at night when the marines fired their flares to keep Charlie at bay, the notion that I might die myself began to recede. The idea that I was a fool, an incompetent, also began to fade as I acquired more and more skill in combat brain surgery. More men left my picnic table/operating room with a fighting chance to live. A professor, a teacher of doctors years ago, once said in one of my classes, "A physician rises to perfection over a pile of corpses." I suppose that was what happened to me. It's disturbing, but that was the reality of it.

Following surgery, the patients would be taken promptly to the intensive care unit, a large tent with the sides rolled up and mosquito netting hanging from the canvas roof edges to the ground. The floor was a plywood platform. Approximately forty patient cots were available to support the needs of the operative and non-operative battle casualties alike. As noted before, by order from the commanding general of the Force Service Support Group Third Marine Division, our holding capacity was very short. More specifically, it was six hours following surgery.

At the designated time, the evacuation helicopters would be brought in, and the patients would be placed aboard (medically stable or not) on stretchers with IV and often blood infusions running, and transferred to to Da Nang airstrip for immediate embarkation to the air force hospital in the Philippines. Once they left on the choppers, we never saw them again.

I seldom had a marine who had been injured in excess of sixty minutes prior to arriving at our facility. Indeed, if it took that long it was usually because the combat zone was under intense enemy fire and the rescue helicopter could not descend to land until the enemy had been suppressed via the ground troops and from the air cover provided by the accompanying gunship. Once the medevac chopper was on the ground, the gunship would hover about twenty-five feet above and fire machine guns in a 360-degree spread near the medevac helo. Once loaded, they both would bolt in a few seconds.

Because we received the patients so quickly after injury, two very visible phenomena were in evidence. First, the magnitude of the injuries were of such a nature that most of us had never seen an individual still breathing after having sustained that magnitude of trauma—they literally did not have time to bleed out. Secondly, the survival rate of the patients increased significantly, again a function of the fact that we got to them before they had a chance to bleed out, in many, many situations.

By way of comparison, statistics recorded during the fighting in France during the course of the First World War revealed that the average casualty reached a field hospital usually in excess of a full forty-eight, and sometimes sixty, hours after injury, thus selecting, so to speak, against those individuals who had severe injuries and could not live that length of time without complex medical care.

In the Second World War, the average time between battle injury and major medical management was still twelve to eighteen hours, whereas in Korea with the introduction of the helicopter, the difference in time between battle injury and formal medical management averaged well under five hours.

In Vietnam the ability of the operational forces to evacuate casualties from the field of battle was significantly enhanced by helicopters. Specifically, the Huey, with its capability of lifting not only a crew of four but sometimes three or four casualties and then dart like a scared cat, was a breakthrough.

The craft could then move very rapidly across the treetops to a military hospital that had been placed as close to the fighting zone as was practical. I had not seen anything like this before. It represented the ultimate in the efficiency of casualty evacuation. It is a given fact that the mortality of battle injuries in Vietnam with the kind of facilities I worked in was well below 5 percent. For this statistical reality, like the other surgeons, I share an element of pride.

I have not uncommonly exclaimed to colleagues and friends that the laudable casualty-management record that we surgeons claimed in Vietnam was just as much a function of the lowly olive-drab helicopter, with its hissing engines and thumping rotor blades, as it was the skill of the many surgeons who cared for the troops.

But with the speed of medevacs also came a previously unobserved and frequently lethal complication in some of the wounded we treated. Fluid collected in the lungs of some patients one or two days after they had undergone resuscitation and appropriate surgery. These unfortunate warriors often died, and for quite a while surgeons couldn't figure out why the soldiers were literally drowning in their own secretions. Eventually, the problem was traced back to the rapid fluid replacement required in individuals who had been rescued so quickly from the field. Similar injuries in previous wars would have led to death before the wounded man reached medical aid. It turned out there was loss of integrity of the lining of the millions of the tiny lung cavities called alveoli. That had never been seen in combat medicine before.

The disorder ultimately was given the name "Da Nang Lung," a condition that later was clearly elucidated at medical centers back in the United States. The mysterious mechanism was confirmed, and effective treatment via an automatic respirator and diuretics was instituted. "Da Nang Lung" is not an uncommon phenomenon seen in badly traumatized patients a day or two after the injury. It is now referred to as ARDS. The acronym refers to adult respiratory distress syndrome, and it remains an ominous and still a frequently lethal complication.

The helicopter medevac system saved lives in Vietnam, but it also had some downsides. "Da Nang Lung" was one of them.

SETTLING IN

I FOUND MYSELF CHANGING AS A man and surgeon during my time in Vietnam, and especially during those first months when I served at Charlie Med. The experience hardened me in a way, but I guess that was natural. Days of boredom and frenetic stress were the norm, but upon some occasions there were moments that stood out more than others. Every soldier has such memories, and sometimes the retelling is painful. Other times the recounting is done with a smile. Life is like that. It is never a case of outright happiness or sadness. It's always a mix, or at least that was how it was for me in 1965 as I cut my teeth as a brain surgeon in the jungles of Vietnam.

There is one incident that I vividly recall, even now. I was in the ICU tent well after midnight during the monsoon season, when the rains were coming straight down. The drops would strike the top of the tent and make a typical muffled sound of water running down the alpine-like roof to mosquito net–covered sides and then splash in the mud. In the distance was the now-routine sound of American artillery rumbling steadily as it always did when Charlie was out and about.

I was in the intensive care unit this particular night, because I had two major head-injury patients who needed my attention in preparation for the helo evacuation slated for 6 a.m. Fatigue was threatening to overcome me. There were two electric lanterns hanging from the peak of the tent, one on either end, and a navy corpsman sitting at one end of the tent on an ammunition crate reconfigured into a desk. His job was to act as intensive care nurse for some thirty to forty patients, lying on cots arrayed along either side of the tent. All other corpsmen were committed to incoming casualties. By way of comparison, intensive care units in the United States consist of about fifteen beds and have at least five fully trained nurses in attendance at all times.

As I sat on the edge of the cot with one of my two head-injury victims, I looked down the line of cots and saw a marine standing with no clothes, his right hand over a wound dressing on the lower right side of the abdomen, and an intravenous infusion running in his left arm. He was simultaneously using his left hand to take the pulse of another casualty patient. I was somewhat struck by this and asked the corpsman in charge what this meant. He indicated that available corpsmen were encumbered elsewhere, and he therefore had taught this marine, who had just had an appendectomy three hours earlier, to take vital signs on his fellow troopers.

I was stunned. Here was an eighteen- or nineteen-year-old kid barely out of surgery, surely in pain and feeling the need to vomit, standing on a cold wet plywood floor in this depressing facility thousands of miles from home. He unhesitatingly rose to the occasion to help a comrade. This marine's willingness, his devotion to duty and beyond, was an inspiration to me. Thinking of him made me figuratively kick myself in the ass. It was quite a while before I felt sorry for myself again.

The helicopter had been introduced in Korea as a fighting platform and as a medical evacuation craft, but in Vietnam the chopper came into its own. Indeed, when you think of that war, it's hard not to conjure up images of the Jolly Green Giants, massive helicopters that were the workhorses of our ground forces. The choppers with which we were most familiar at Charlie Med were much smaller.

Simply referred to as the Huey, these versatile helicopters were dull olive drab and were about twenty-five feet long with skids. The cabin was about eighteen inches above the ground. Two pilots sat in front with a panoramic bubble-shaped windshield. There was an observer seat just behind and between them. The back part of the cabin was larger, accommodating two gunner crewmen, each manning a mounted machine gun on either side. The cabin could carry about three or four additional men if necessary. Side doors in the back slid open, providing excellent visibility. Mounted outside each side of the Huey were both machine guns and rocket launchers fixed to the craft. The engine (replaced soon after with two engines) was mounted above the cabin with the rotor blades above it.

The performance of these choppers was impressive. They could jump into the air and go forward or sideways or climb with ease, and they could hit top speeds of 110 miles per hour. Medevac Hueys were not armed to save on space and weight; however, they always traveled with an armed craft. Flying often at less than one hundred feet at 110 mph, they can attack a target or rescue a wounded marine, maybe three or four, and then scurry away.

I had no experience with the mechanism of emergency air transport, specifically via helicopter, until I arrived in Vietnam. When a marine ground unit engaged the enemy and sustained casualties, one member of the unit, who carried a radio on his backpack, immediately summoned the medevac over the specified radio frequency and provided the appropriate ground coordinates. The time it took from this radio call to the dispatcher at the marine helicopter base was, of course, practically instantaneous.

The helicopter crews were always sitting in the adjacent ready room, a tent, and they would note the coordinates, run promptly to their aircraft, and within five plus minutes they were airborne. Since the choppers could travel through the air at either treetop or five hundred-foot altitude, and considering the fact that much of the combat took place well inside of thirty miles from medical facilities, one can appreciate how quickly the helicopter made its way to the scene.

Then with the fire support provided by the marines on the ground and the gunship partner, the medevac chopper descended quickly to the ground, the side-door crewmen jumped out, and with or without the aid of the combatant marines on the ground, they dragged or carried the wounded up to the craft, shoved them on the flat platform-like inner cabin floor (about 18 to 24 inches off the ground), and then hopped back on board. The pilots could lift off in less than ten seconds and head back to us. Finally, the pilots radioed ahead that casualties were coming in, and we'd all get ready for the next round of carnage.

Typically at C-Med we were within thirty to forty yards from the helo pad and could hear and see one coming in. If not in the OR with a previous case, we quickly congregated in the shock tent adjacent to the helo pad and helped extract patients from the helo, placed them on stretchers, and carried them to the shock tent, where we placed the stretcher on two sawhorses and began immediate care. It was quite an efficient way to handle casualties, more so than in any other previous war.

Getting used to the choppers and the rapid pace of the OR when casualties streamed in, I had to come to grips with the fact that the Viet Cong were often lurking about. Shortly after I arrived on the compound, I was advised that the enemy frequently approached to within five hundred yards of the oval perimeter around us. Therefore interposed between the compound and the potential zone of hostility were the series of foxholes manned by marines. They would rotate with a partner such that there was twenty-four-hour-a-day presence in each of the foxholes. This was less than seventy-five yards from our tents.

Routinely, one could hear rifle fire from one or another of these security positions, often during the day but more particularly during the night when shadows took form and nerves were frayed. Shooting then was heard at least two to three times per hour from one of the foxholes. We had on board the hospital compound a marine lieutenant who was in charge of this security force and whose obligation it was to creep out to each of the foxholes, especially during the nighttime to ensure that the marines were not asleep but manning their posts, and that they had not been surreptitiously overcome by the enemy. Under such a scenario the enemy could steal through that position and onto our compound with obvious results.

Late one night, I was attempting to sleep on my cot in a tent that I shared with five other officers. Sleepless and jittery, I heard footsteps creeping through the brush very nearby. The canvas on the sides of the tent had been rolled up about four feet from the ground for ventilation. As the footsteps came closer, I could see the individual's legs and boots in the moonlight as he proceeded along the side of my tent closer to my location.

As I had been advised, I quietly picked up my loaded .45-caliber handgun and, thinking that the figure walking slowly in my direction was an enemy infiltrator, pointed the weapon directly at him. He was not less than eight feet away. I resolved that if he angled his path toward me I would have to shoot him.

He did not, however, and continued to walk slowly by, beyond the tent and out of earshot. I am sure I waited an hour before I put the weapon back on the plywood floor adjacent to my cot and then, rather than asleep, wondered the rest of the night as to who that was, where he was going, and where he came from.

The following morning, as was the routine, a staff meeting took place. This included surgeons, medical service corps officers who were basically administrators of the compound, and the one marine security officer in charge of the marine security force. We met in a medium-sized tent with plywood floors, a few wooden benches, and a portable chalkboard at the front. The major points of discussion revolved around the casualty volume and management that had developed in the previous twenty-four hours, including, available supplies, times of evacuation, condition of the staff, and matters of such.

Toward the end of the meeting, the officer in charge asked if there were any questions from the hospital staff members. I raised my hand and brought to his attention what had occurred during the previous night and also indicated that I had pointed my weapon at whomever that was. As if he had been jolted from his position on the wooden bench by an electric charge, the marine security officer literally vaulted to a standing position, tripped over his bench, and addressed me forcefully, and in a pleading fashion, eyes wide open and clearly shaken.

"Lieutenant Pitlyk, sir! It is my responsibility to patrol

the compound, sir! Including near your tent, sir! Please don't shoot me, sir!"

My cheeks went red with the heat of a blush. My colleagues smiled and shook their heads, and others laughed out loud. I felt like an idiot. I strongly suspect the security officer wanted me dead. I remained seated as I assured him that I promised not to blow his head off in the middle of the night. Somehow the important bit of information about the nightly patrols had not been communicated to me when I came on board. The marines called mistakes like this "the fog of war." In my case, it had been pretty funny. In other cases, the end result was a fatality due to friendly fire.

In between the carnage and boredom, there were some amusing moments. One involved a happening at the toilet facilities. Typically, since there was no plumbing available in these field units, a round hole approximately ten feet in diameter is dug to a depth of about five feet. On top of the hole is then placed a knee-high oval wood cylinder that is slightly larger in diameter than the hole so that it fits directly on top of it without falling in. The top of this cylinder is covered with a flat, wooden platform that is cut into a round disk and positioned directly over the cylinder to form a hat-like structure. Then four holes (toilet seats) are cut in the periphery of this round disk at ninety degrees with respect to each other.

The entire structure was then enclosed in a medium-sized standard military tent. This represented the field toilet arrangements whereby four individuals could defecate or urinate at one time. There was no extra charge for splinters in the seats. Each day the tent would be temporarily removed, the disk-like top with the four small openings was lifted off, and diesel oil was poured into the hole and then ignited so as to afford some semblance of sanitation. What an odor!

One day a marine, who was hospitalized with malaria

and was somewhat confused, walked out of the ICU tent into the field lavatory, somehow lifted the disk-like lid over the hole and fell in. Needless to say, there was a great deal of commotion around the compound as to how this happened. After he was extricated, a couple of unfortunate corpsmen were detailed with the responsibility of cleaning him up.

In late December, the monsoon season began with rain falling daily and on some occasions for many hours at a time. Since much of the ground in our compound had been cleared of brush and vegetation, the soil became soft and muddy so that when we walked, our boots would sink frequently below our ankles. The foxholes that all of us were required to dig just outside of our tents were filled with water, and on one occasion I saw one of the physicians with a bar of soap, sitting naked in the hole surrounded by muddy water, taking a tub bath.

At around Christmas, my tent mates and I decided that we should have a tree. We found a small tree of some sort near the edge of the compound, cut it down, and brought it into the tent with the intent of promoting a Christmas atmosphere. After erecting it in a secure standing position with some effort, we chose to decorate it in a holiday fashion.

Certainly no such thing as tree lights, ornaments, tinsel, or other paraphernalia was available, so we were required to be creative. We took lids from C-ration cans, punched a little hole at the edge, tied a string through the holes, and hung them on the branches as ornaments. Then we took pieces of cardboard from supply containers, cut them in three- to four-inch squares, tied a string on the corner, and after inscribing phrases that were of a surly and obscene nature (hardly fit for print), we hung them also as ornaments on our tree. Although the result bordered on blasphemy at this sacred time of the year, it was our position that the Lord would forgive us in the view of circumstances.

At Charlie Med we did not have showers. The only recourse was to sponge ourselves with a bucket of water procured from the area near the ICU. I, for one, was really frustrated about the lack of showers, so a tent mate and I concocted an idea to remedy the problem. The enterprise was worthy of planning a major offensive. We tracked down a fifty-gallon oil drum abandoned by the Sea Bees, took off the lid from one end, and then with some crude nails we found a piece of a two-by-four for a hammer. We punched multiple nail holes in the central part of the bottom of the drum in the design of a showerhead. We then carried the oil drum to a local tree, of which there were several on the compound, wedged it in the branches six-plus feet above ground such that the open shower holes, so to speak, would face directly downward. We then tracked down some wire cable and secured the drum to the tree trunk, limb and support frame. Finally, with other pieces of two-by-fours and pine boards that had been left over from the equipment boxes abandoned by the Sea Bees (following construction of the hospital), we were able to build a very crude stairway with about five steps up to the midpoint of the fifty-gallon oil drum.

Well aware that at the end of the chow line in the evening there were three forty-gallon cans of heated water used for cleansing the mess trays, the two of us would wait around until the end of chow and then swipe the third or last container of heated water, which was the cleanest since it was the third one to have mess trays dipped and swirled around in it. Struggling and slipping, we then carried the water can across the often-muddy path to our makeshift shower in the tree. Before ascending the tree we took off all our clothes, wrestled the can of heated water up the rickety old stairway, poured it into our shower container, and quickly jumped up the stairs and hustled, first one and then the other, under the dripping warm water, during which time we quickly soaped ourselves up, rinsed ourselves, and made room for the second man.

The system worked very well. Except for the chilly, rainy nights when we ran naked, carrying our clothes back to our housing tents, we found this showering mechanism to be a touch of class.

The daily events at this marine facility continued with unending oncoming helicopters laden with battered troops silhouetted against the backdrop of clouds, rain, mud, and the constant thunder of artillery in the distance and frequent rifle fire from our marine guards in the foxholes nearby. They did not hesitate to fire into the wooded surroundings about 150 yards from our tents, lest the VC, in cover of brush or darkness, crawl in and gun down our staff.

In December 1965, there were about 250,000 troops in Vietnam. The battle plan for the marines was "sweep and destroy," which meant a hundred or so would be ferried into the jungle to clear a designated zone of the VC and then return via Hueys to their garrison. There were no clear front lines. Indeed, most of the war was guerrilla fighting.

Frequent rifle fire from the marines in the periphery foxholes, shooting at either real or imagined enemy movements in the trees, helped punctuate the sounds of the air force and marine jet fighter bombers taking off from the nearby Da Nang airstrip, laden with their deadly load of bombs and napalm. They created an earsplitting roar as they streaked overhead, sometimes less than five hundred feet above us. All these many sounds composed a symphony of fear while the casualties continued to flow in.

On occasion, a young marine would be evacuated to us in "shell shock." I observed one of these one night carried off the helicopter, lying on a stretcher with no wounds; his eyes, however, were open and staring directly forward, yet communicating no recognition or awareness of his surroundings. Curiously, one could stick a needle into his arm, hand, or foot, and he would not move, grimace, or in any fashion acknowledge recognition of discomfort. In my limited exposure to the field of psychiatry in medical school, I had heard of such things; however, directly observing a victim of this disorder was an impressive and disturbing experience.

As I looked at this young man, I could only imagine what had driven him into this mind-set—or, I should say, out of his mind. One could imagine day after day, night after night, he and his comrades in arms would be sent out on either small patrols of twelve or so men or become part of a larger search-and-destroy operation, where a company-size group (two hundred men) would move into the jungle, searching for the enemy while creeping through the thick brush between the land mines that could take off an individual's legs up to his hips in a flash. Enemy troops in groups or snipers hidden in the brush might appear in an instant with withering fire, or they might hurl hand grenades. Other hazards also existed.

On one occasion, a king cobra snake sprang up from the brush directly in front of the lead man on patrol, its elongated body coiled on the ground while it extended its upper body and neck, with the typical wide flared hood for which they are noted pointed directly at the face of the stunned marine in a menacing fashion. The man directly behind him instinctively raised his rifle, fired, and killed the reptile in an instant. Indeed, the overwhelming impact of such onerous traumatic experiences is easily appreciated. Why we saw such emotionally shattered troops only infrequently was something of a wonder.

If the troops complete their mission and have not been disabled, they return to their home base, a paltry jungle clearing with foxholes and pup tents, for a twenty-four-hour period or so, during which time they can clean their weapons, replenish their ammunition supplies, eat C rations, and prepare for the next patrol.

I often thought while I was in Vietnam, and I still think today, that I would never have had the personal courage to expose myself to the daily intense risk that the men I treated endured for thirteen months. The tour of duty required by every marine who went to Vietnam was about as demanding as it got, and I admired the fighting men who were brave enough to go through it. I still can recall the remark of a senior marine figure during my brief military indoctrination at Camp Pendleton Marine Base. He said we train our troops to be more fearful of us than the enemy

After weeks on end at our facility, my feeling of anxiety and personal fear diminished somewhat and was replaced by a sense of guilt and embarrassment prompted by the fact that I was stationed at a semi-secure area and not required to crawl out into the enemy's homeland night after night, knowing the hazards. Although I did not discuss it with my colleagues, I have the notion that many of them underwent a comparable evolution of this facet of emotions, particularly after observing the psychiatric casualties.

Communication with the outside world was quite limited. However, orders coming from headquarters to us were daily events, and these addressed such things as casualty levels, supply reserves, staff adequacy, and the like. As far as how the war was going, we didn't have a clue, except for what we saw firsthand. There was no Internet. There were no cell phones. We had no television or the 1965 equivalent of CNN. We just focused on the discharge of our responsibilities to care for the wounded. One or two of the physicians had a small portable radio that could pick up only one station, a demoralizing broadcast from North Vietnam aimed at depressing us even more than we might be already.

The radio personality was a woman who we nicknamed "Hanoi Hanna." She persistently said that the American effort was fruitless, counterproductive, and was only successful in destroying innocent people. During this propaganda, she often said those we had left back in the United States were pursuing their own personal ambitions, including gradually forgetting the men in Vietnam.

Disturbingly, she knew names of some of the individuals, including some in our compound. She would speak directly to them by name and advised them that their wives or girlfriends were seeing other men back in the United States. We often wondered how she was able to obtain the names and even the home records of these American servicemen. This was one aspect of her broadcasts that our staff considered a matter of concern. It conveyed the impression that the enemy had an informer at our hospital. Her voice was far from irritating or obnoxious. Indeed, it was soft, pleasant, and womanly. I'm sorry to say Hanoi Hanna did make some of us feel really bad, but I guess it was our own fault for even listening to her.

As the holidays came and went, I almost forgot that I was only temporarily assigned to Charlie Med. I'd made some good friends, especially with my CO, Commander Greg Grew, a man I connected closely with for many years after the war. I'd been sent deep "in-country" to help save lives in the most primitive conditions imaginable, and after my initial horror, frustration, fear, and self-doubt, I'd managed to find a sort of equilibrium, a way to cope. I wasn't always successful, but I did see improvement in both my emotional outlook and in my technical skill as a neurosurgeon.

Then marching orders from HQ came in mid-January

1966, one short year since I'd set off on my own to build a prosperous private practice and ended up being drawn to Vietnam. So much had changed. It seemed that repairs to the naval hospital that had been overrun and destroyed were about finished, and the navy brass wanted me down in Da Nang to serve on the medical staff, as was originally planned.

I did not shed any tears as I packed my seabag and footlocker, but I did know my time at Charlie Med had tested me to the limit. It had stripped away any of the soft stateside veneer that I'd come with and replaced it all with a thick skin. I just hoped it would be thick enough for whatever Vietnam had in store for me next.

Vietnamese farmer

Basic helicopter (Huey)

Operating Room Charlie Med. Surrounding sandbags offer protection from incoming mortars

Air force casualty-evacuation plane loading patients for trip to air force hospital in Philippines

Charlie Med viewed from helicopter landing pad

Charlie Med shower

9

CHINA BEACH

THE OLIVE-DRAB "SIX-BY" (THE COMMON TERM for a heavy military truck) idled in the center of the Charlie Med compound, the driver of the truck waiting patiently for me to get the last of my things together for the ride back toward Da Nang and the G-4 hospital, where I'd spend the next phase of my tour of duty in Vietnam. When I'd said my last good-byes to my tent mates, I hurried outside, ran up to the truck, and threw my seabag and a small box of operative reports in the back. I jumped in and the driver took off.

As the truck lumbered along and bounced its cargo back and forth (me included), I compared and contrasted the positive and negative facets of my results over the preceding ten weeks. The conclusion was that they had been less than satisfactory. Curiously, even though I still harbored a negative image of my ability, it was not as profound now. Sure, I could have been more effective if I'd had more experience before finding myself plunked down in a war zone at Charlie Med. I could have done better if I'd had the right equipment, or even a primitive OR instead of the picnic table I'd used on occasion.

I initially thought the marines I operated on were best left to be cared for by the air force hospital neurosurgeon in the Philippines. But I quickly realized that many of the kids would have died if I'd declined to take a chance and try to save them. The flight time to Manila was about five hours, and many of my patients could not tolerate such a delay. In a sense, I think I was rationalizing, and I had plenty of time to do it as the truck lurched and lumbered down the road toward Da Nang.

A voice hammered away in my head, threatening to drown out my seemingly reasonable justifications for operating on kids when I knew deep down I lacked the experience. *Why did the navy allow such incompetence? Why did the navy let me do it?* Just as quickly I heard in my head the calm authoritative voice of Commander Grew: "You treated many and some died, but if you had not come, they all would have died."

I thought about what Grew had said for a long time, and I finally had to admit to myself that he was right. It didn't absolve me of the guilt I felt, but it did make the hurt a little less painful. I began to wonder what the hospital I was going to would be like. Would it have new operating room facilities, including lighting and equipment support? Would I actually be allowed to use the operating room for the moderately long neurosurgical procedures I had to carry out to save wounded marines? Would postoperative ICU facilities be better than those at Charlie Med?

"Oh, God!" I whispered to myself. "What if it's worse?" What if I was asked to do surgery in a field kitchen on a wooden table with flashlights for illumination and imagination for sterility? What if I was forced to ship patients out after only six hours at the new hospital, whether they were stable or not, even if they were too seriously wounded to travel? So many of the men were taken from my care so quickly that I had no idea what happened to the kids I tried to save. I fear many died simply because of the way the field hospital was directed to treat patients, as if they were like cattle being fed into a machine to be chewed up, patched up, and then spit out as fast as possible.

The jungle-colored truck continued bouncing over the single-lane road, snaking its way downward from the slightly elevated position of Charlie Med. We moved slowly out of the intense fertile jungle environment toward the sea level region near the city of Da Nang. The foliage became much less dense as we neared the coast. The truck lumbered, rocked, and bumped until I thought my head would fall off, but I was still happy to be there. I was happy to have Charlie Med behind me, though I was also anxious about what was in store for me next.

We soon circled around a portion of Da Nang Harbor, in which one could see several large naval supply ships riding at anchor. One or two others were under way, either entering the harbor to bring in more supplies and equipment or exiting, destined for the sea, empty, riding higher in the water and heading for a port of resupply in the United States, a long way off. The road before us narrowed down to one lane as we approached the rapid flowing muddy waterway called the Da Nang River, originating in the highlands to the west, racing down across the flatlands, and then rushing into the harbor and ultimately out to sea.

The river was about half a mile wide and had been spanned by the Sea Bees by means of a pontoon bridge. Such a bridge is a series of what ostensibly appeared to be long narrow rowboats about eighteen feet long, which were lashed together side by side until they spanned the entire river width. The length of each pontoon was parallel to the rapidly flowing water. Across this floating pontoon array was stretched flexible metal perforated sheeting that was the width of a one-lane road and connected piece by piece from one side of the river to the other, thus forming a floating bridge. In a way, it looked like a large caterpillar.

The truck came to a stop, waiting for traffic from the other direction to complete its journey across, at which point we were given the green flag to proceed by a marine standing with a rifle slung over his shoulder, helmet in place, and flak jacket securely fastened. His face was deeply tanned and expressionless. The heavy truck crept up onto the floating bridge that literally would undulate in the water with the weight of the vehicle as it moved slowly across from pontoon to pontoon. Now this animal was wiggling and truly mimicked the movements of a long crawling caterpillar or snake. If a tank was anywhere on the bridge, its enormous weight would amplify the undulations of the roadway.

I noticed that about every twenty-five paces along the bridge facing upstream was a rifleman firing frequently at what appeared to be floating lily pads, some even with blooms in the center of them. These pads were quite numerous and most attractive. Indeed, I counted at least fifty to sixty flowing downward with the water to the bridge and then either touching and bouncing off the pontoon supports or flowing between the two, on downward and out into the bay. It became obvious to me that the marines were shooting at each of these for reasons that were other than target practice. At this point in my tour in the country, I was growing accustomed to various peculiar ways of doing things. Only later after I had arrived at the naval hospital some ten miles further was I advised that these so-called floating water lilies often harbored a Viet Cong–planted dynamite package that, like a land mine, exploded on contact and could, of course, destroy the bridge and drown those who happened to be on board. By shooting each one some fifty to sixty yards before they touched the bridge, a rifleman would hopefully explode these devices and prevent such a calamity.

Having crossed the bridge, we again resumed our course on a two-lane road that now distinctly coursed through a more sandy and arid countryside. We passed Vietnamese villages that seemed to encompass about two hundred people living in thatched huts and busily moving about, oblivious to the military vehicles moving along the road. As the truck moved along, we occasionally would come to what is called a "checkpoint," where armed marines waited, stopped the vehicle, confirmed the driver's identification, looked in the back to confirm I was not a Viet Cong infiltrator, and then allowed us to move on.

Other vehicles on the road going either way included trucks of various sizes, jeeps, and an occasional marine tank that seemed to take up the whole road and make an enormous amount of noise, in addition to leaving a trail of smoke that had the odor of an aggregate of about eight city buses.

It was dry and partly sunny, and the temperature was not unpleasant. On either side of the roadway was concertina wire. Beyond these fences, I was advised later, were scattered land mines to protect against infiltrators, particularly at night. As the truck rumbled on, I could see the South China Sea off to the east about two miles. To the west I could look up into the jungle region from whence I had come. We slowed and stopped for another checkpoint, confirmed our authenticity to an expressionless sunburned marine, and then were allowed to move on.

After about two more miles we passed a marine helicopter base enshrouded in barbed wire. Olive-drab helicopters sat like a swarm of hornets on the ground. Others were taking off and landing, always in pairs. From a distance they looked like angry bees. This base was called MAG 16, which stands for Marine Air Group 16. As we drove along the rickety road, we found ourselves distinctly on sandy surface with virtually no foliage to be seen. Off on the right we approached a large assemblage of Quonset huts organized in neat parallel rows, occupying approximately thirty-plus acres and surrounded again by the now-familiar concertina wire. Just peripheral to this wire were again marked-off mine fields. The truck turned into the entrance gate manned by two armed marines who carefully interrogated the driver, inspected the vehicle, and looked at my set of orders. With seeming reluctance they let us in. The truck proceeded slowly through the wide-hinged, crudely built gate covered with concertina wire, which was closed behind us by the marine guards. The driver drove slowly up to one of the Quonset huts identified with a stenciled sign above the door that read "NSA Hospital Administration."

I was grateful that this less-than-comfortable ride had come to an end, and I climbed over the railing on the back of the truck, stepped down on one of the truck's tires, and navigated the rest of the way by jumping to the ground.

I took a moment to gaze around at my new home. The surface of the ground was entirely sand. Not a tree or a blade of grass was to be seen. Quonset huts were numerous. Nearby was the helicopter landing platform, and adjacent to this was another Quonset, the shock hut. It opened directly toward the helicopter pad. The internal configuration, like the one at the marine field hospital, was arranged to include sawhorses on either side of a central aisle, extending from one end of the Quonset to the other. Casualties on stretchers were placed across these for emergency care like at Charlie Med.

The distance from the end of the Quonset to a landing

helicopter was less than twenty-five yards. On the other end of the shock tent were three Quonsets arranged in a parallel fashion with wood walkways from the entrance on either end. These walkways connected the shock Quonsets to the two surgery Quonsets and to the ICU Quonset and ward Quonsets. In this way a wounded person could be transported with ease on a rolling stretcher called a "gurney", from the shock tent to surgery and from surgery to other patient care Quonsets. In addition, there were Quonsets for pharmacy, X-ray, ICU, and general care (malaria, infections, depression, etc.).

Beyond this kaleidoscope of medical-management Quonsets were the structures needed for maintenance and support of the personnel on the compound, including housing, laundry facilities, administration, sterilization facilities, food preparation, and dining facilities. This place was at least fifteen times larger than Charlie Med, and I estimated that about two hundred people were assigned to the hospital, including about twenty-five doctors. Where Charlie Med was a maze of tents, this place was mass of Quonset Huts.

While I was still just standing there taking in the sights, a marine came up to me, saluted, and said he was to escort me to my permanent lodgings, another Quonset about two hundred yards from the patient-care zone. Upon entering my new digs, I noticed immediately that the Quonset was dimly lit and that no provision had been made for a desk. Later, I built my own desk out of discarded wooden crates, but at that moment the obvious continuation of primitive conditions got me down a bit. I also noticed that there was sand everywhere, and I wondered how it got inside. I soon learned that blowing sand would work its way up from beneath the plywood floor. On days when I felt depressed and lonely, I'd reopen a letter to reread it and out would come grains of sand. We would find it in our boots in the morning or in our khaki-colored uniforms that had hung for a day or so next to our rack. There was very little air circulation through these Quonsets. As is traditional on military facilities, another Quonset hut with a plywood floor beneath it was offered to us as an officers' club.

Emotional escape was provided by this officers' club, which was near our sleeping Quonsets and in which was a bar at one corner, several stools, a generous display of various types of liquor, and a few chairs and tables on the wooden plank floor. Metal chairs and a few crude wood tables were included for our use when relaxing.

This club was used extensively during my tour there and indeed was a haven, an oasis from the turmoil. A mixed drink was fifteen cents. Beer was a dime. Discussions among the physicians and the Medical Service Corps officers here frequently lingered on into the late evening. Commonly a motion picture was brought to us and would be shown in the "O club" after dark in the evening. It represented a curious diversion even for the most intellectually gifted of our group. The most interesting thing about the movies was the fact that the film reel often would break at some point in the presentation. This prompted comical remarks from the attendees.

The latrines included the notorious "four holer" (common term for a field toilet), flies included. Curiously this structure provided subject matter for light banter. In addition, the Sea Bees provided several angled pieces of narrow pipe at various locations of the hospital compound that were called "piss tubes." They were about three feet high and stuck out from the sand. Thanks to the male anatomy, they were amazingly convenient.

This entire village of Quonset huts was known as China Beach and was spread over several acres of sand on a gentle slope, leading a couple miles downward toward the South China Sea. We were far enough away so that we could not hear the surf, but it was somehow nice to know the beach was there. The compound was surrounded by concertina wire just inside of which were a series of strategically placed five-foot holes in the sand, the rims of which were surrounded by a row of filled sandbags. These holes were arranged at about seventy- to eighty-yard intervals well within sight of each other and surrounded the entire perimeter of the hospital compound. In each hole were stationed two marines armed with rifles and a means of radio communication with their leader on the hospital grounds.

In the center of the compound was a mortar tube placed on level ground, surrounded by filled sandbags such that a crouching marine could see up over the top of the bags but would be reasonably protected from rifle fire coming from outside the concertina wire. The two-man mortar crew could monitor the western (most vulnerable side) of the fence line at all times. Finally a tank prowled the fence line at night. Evidently the marines had no intention of allowing the Viet Cong a second chance to lay waste to our hospital, but that somehow didn't reassure me much.

Just about three hundred yards west of the hospital compound, the ground sloped downward toward the fast-flowing Da Nang River, which was thought to be the main route of enemy guerrilla assaults. The Viet Cong would hide in small river craft called "sampans," which were about sixteen feet long semi-canoe structures with thatched roofs on the top and ordinarily used by natives for transportation of foodstuffs and the like up and down the river to and from market. On occasions, however, such a sampan was either commandeered or volunteered for Viet Cong use and would hide several troops and a mortar tube. They could float down the river at dusk, pull off to the side in the proximity of our hospital, charge up the sandy incline, and assault the compound. Such was the case ten days prior to my arrival.

That night, they came at dusk, up from the river, about thirty-five strong. Clad in scanty clothing and carrying both satchel charges and automatic weapons, they darted directly for the main hospital buildings. Their targets were the ORs, X-ray facility, sterile supply, and pharmacy. A satchel charge was tossed into each Quonset followed by a burst from an automatic weapon. Seeing no occupants and having achieved their objective, they retreated back to the river and their sampans. The element of surprise was perfect, and the time required was about ten minutes! They knew precisely what they wanted to destroy and did it. Now the Quonsets were completely replaced; ORs, pharmacy, and the sterilizer were reestablished; and the X-ray facility was again operating, although bullet holes from automatic weapons remained in the outer covering of the X-ray control console and indeed were present for as long as I was at China Beach.

One of my initial impressions of the place was the surreal nature of it all. It was different from Charlie Med, of course, but each was uniquely insane in its own way. Every night the sun settled beyond the jungle-laden highlands to the west, and a brief twilight would be replaced by the darkness. Once this set in, nature was cheated out of the seclusion usually provided by night by the ever-present and continuous illumination of aerial flares dropped from aircraft. In association with the night were the sounds of the country. In some ways, it was a macabre musical symphony with the underlying theme or beat being the frequent, distant rumble of outgoing artillery. Superimposed upon this would be less frequent, intermittent, sharp, high-frequency shots of rifle fire and automatic weapons directed at shadows in the night, which sometimes were real but often just imagined.

The overriding harmonic in this melody of death was the

increasing crescendo of the UH-1 helicopter coming over a distant hill at a relatively low speed, heading for our hospital with one to three casualties on board. First, the helicopter could be barely heard in the distance as a low *thump, thump, thump* that increased in crescendo as the craft approached the hospital landing pad. Then, as it swooped low over the Quonsets, the crescendo of the sound increased to an intense tempo, not unlike a Beethoven symphony rising in volume with the basic pulsating sounds of the whirling helicopter blades and the hissing of the jet engines. This was like a background of violins and a harmony of five flutes. The background noise with the superimposed staccato of a helicopter swooping in was such a common occurrence that many personnel not involved in patient care ignored the sound.

For the surgeons, the throbbing noise of an incoming helicopter late at night most frequently meant they would be dredged up from sleep by a corpsman sent over from the shock Quonset to report another one to five casualties. I'm sure that it was only a paranoid perception; however, it seemed to me that 80 percent of those incoming helicopters in the night were carrying head injuries.

To hear birds chirping, crickets echoing, owls, prairie dogs, or any other form of animal life meant that you were dreaming, intoxicated, or mentally decompensated. Realistically, this was probably due to the high volume of noise created by the artillery, the automatic weapons, and the helicopters, all echoing decibels at a magnitude such that we simply suppressed all nocturnal sounds of nature.

When I was a child and was awake at night for one reason or another, it seemed that the length of the night was interminable. Indeed, being summoned to the shock Quonset after midnight resurrected in my mind these childhood prolonged frightful nights. We humans are basically not nocturnal and find ourselves competing with our emotions to act dispassionately or with even an element of candor when called upon to discharge complicated mental and technical skills in the middle of the night.

Although I never discussed this concept with my colleagues, there is clearly an emotional distinction during the course of diagnostic evaluations and operative surgery after dark as compared to the same in daylight. To put it in the vernacular, we were cranky at night. It seemed (and I was most grateful for the phenomenon) that, once I was fully awake and had a chance to evaluate the patient and then progressed to the moment of surgery, my level of awareness and attitude mimicked that during daytime. It was not uncommon during an operation at "zero dark thirty" to again hear the pulsating drone of a helo, first at a very low decibel and then ever increasing in intensity as it approached our base. Each time I was well aware that this could be yet another neurosurgical problem to be deposited on our metaphorical doorstep.

I will not deny that with such an occurrence an element of dismay would come over me. However, being the only neurosurgeon for hundreds of miles, I could not dare project my true feelings to my colleagues or subordinates lest a similar sense of resentment become contagious.

Following completion of an operation, it was necessary to follow along with the corpsmen as they moved this patient from the operating Quonset thirty yards or so along the wooden walkways between Quonsets to the intensive care unit, where I would spend another half hour monitoring the injured marine, writing postoperative orders, and taking a quick peek at the usual three or four other cases I had in there from the last one or two days of surgery.

If at this point the patient looked relatively stable, I would walk across the sand dunes toward the housing

Quonset. It was my policy to routinely stop at the officers' club, walk in, turn on a dim light, and listen to music for a while, usually tapes of Barbra Streisand. Her voice seemed to capture my emotional need at the moment. Although somewhat sad, it also projected an element of dynamism that clearly boosted my morale. When the tape was over, I would turn out the light and go to my bunk. Such was navigated at night generally without difficulty, thanks to the ever-present aerial flares. I'd walk carefully across the plywood floor of the Quonset so as not to awaken the half-dozen other medical officers and work my way to my own bunk.

Often I'd simply fall upon it facedown, making no attempt to remove my uniform or boots, and awaken on a bright morning alone, all my roommates having gone earlier. The irregular, chaotic, nocturnal neurosurgical practice I regretfully was developing soon became a very common and almost routine agenda for me. I pondered why so many neurosurgical cases came in the middle of the night as opposed to the daytime, yet to this day I do not know. Somehow, I suspect it was related to marine operational planning for the combat zone. Of course, such was never shared with me.

Many years have distanced me from that far-off land. Even now when called out in the middle of the night, there is sometimes a sensation of déjà vu, recalling again those long sardonic faces on physicians and corpsman alike, moving like robots from our cots to the ORs. Even now I can imagine the early-morning beard shadows on the faces coupled with the tired, almost sunken, and darkened eyes, coupled with the completely flat affect that typified all who participated in so many midnight melodramas.

I made many attempts to minimize my remorse and my own stress. When I thought about it, I had to agree that the injured trooper was the only person who had a right to develop depression or personal resentment. We, the medical providers, simply had to, in a Pavlovian fashion, provide the diagnostic skill and surgical talent for which we had been trained, after which we could return to our sleeping area and lie down on a dry, relatively safe bunk. We could possibly even expect to sleep from three to eight hours without interruption—never so fortunate the marine!

This little course in self-administered psychotherapy did not always suffice, however, and night after night at four or five o'clock in the morning after completing a case and listening to music before the first fingers of the dawn pointed to the eastern sky, I'd return to my sleeping area, simply wondering when the next casualties would arrive. The ominous *thump, thump, thump* of chopper blades was a sad symphony that went on and on.

Sampans on Da Nang River

Operating Room China Beach. Note foxhole near entrance and sandbags to afford some protection from incoming mortars

Operating Room China Beach one day after Viet Cong attack and overrun

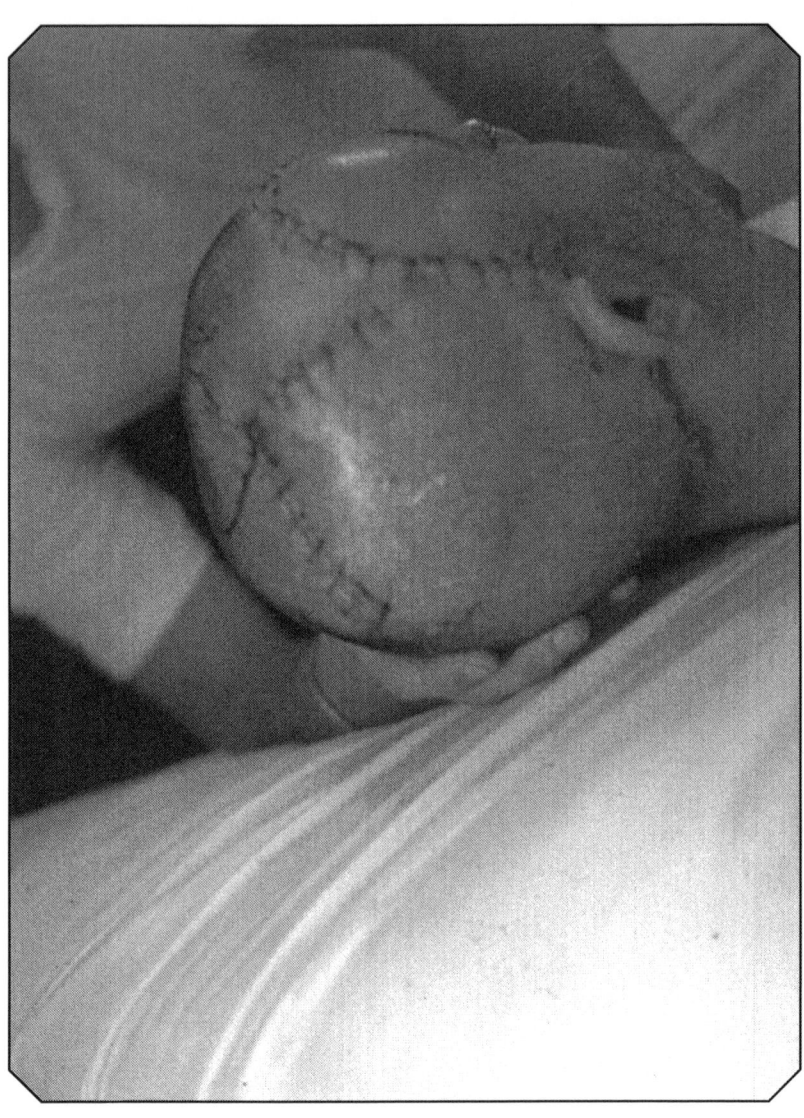
Marine victim of blast injury to head (postoperative)

Bullet hole in helmet removed from wounded marine. China Beach

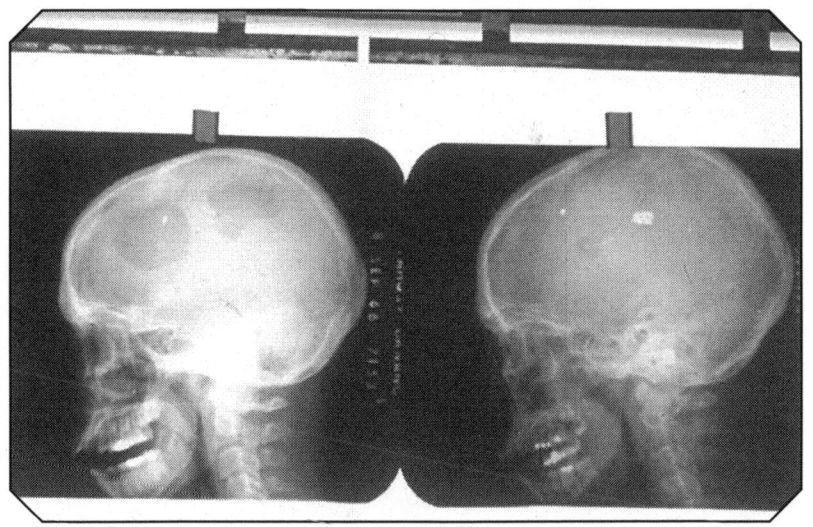

Preoperative (right) and postoperative (left) skull X-ray showing removal of land mine fragments from marine victim. China Beach

Operating Room scene China Beach (note multiple surgeon involvement)

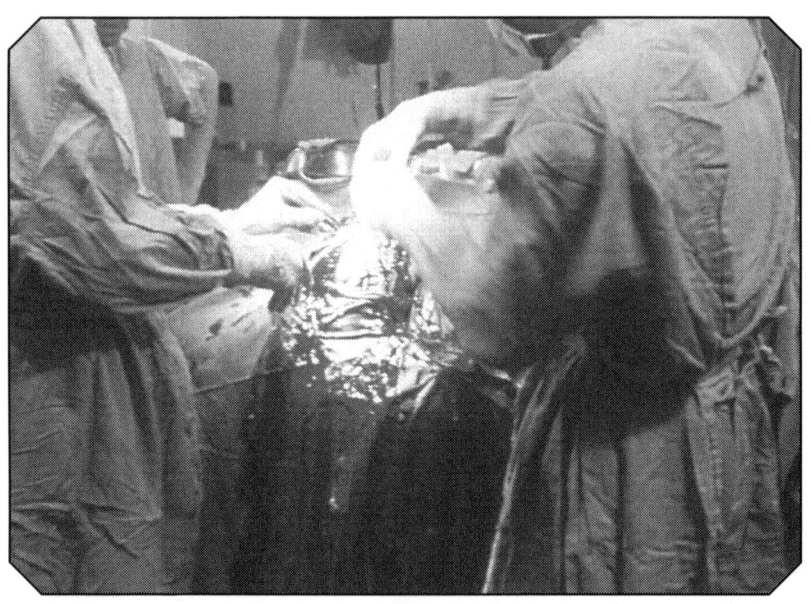

Neurosurgical operation in progress. China Beach

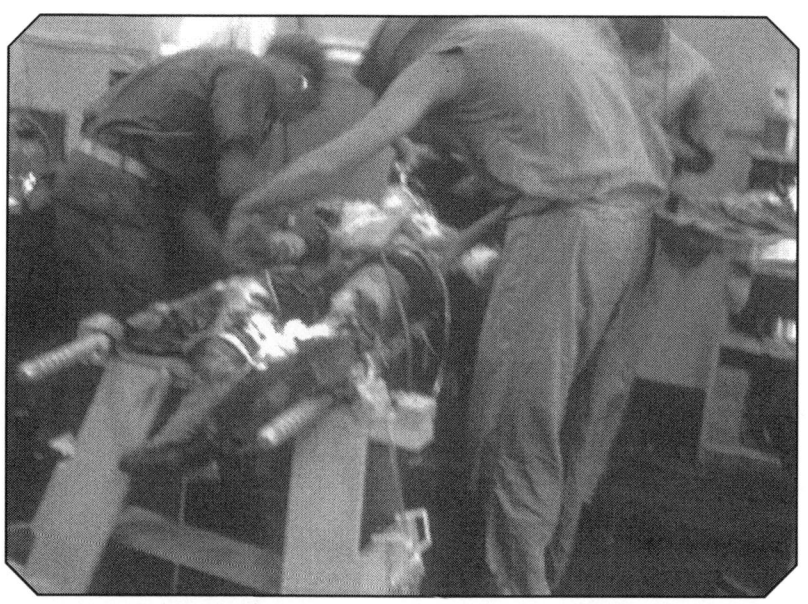

Marine casualty undergoing resuscitation in shock Quonset. China Beach

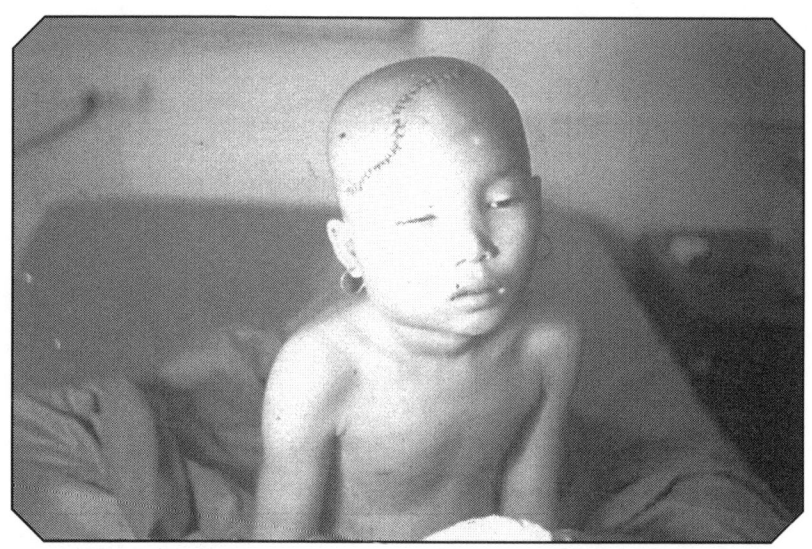

Child, postoperative, following brain injury operation. China Beach

View of China Beach looking toward South China Sea

10

SUPPLY AND DEMAND

FOLLOWING THE TRUCK RIDE AND THE tour of the new hospital, I was introduced to Captain Canada, the commanding officer of China Beach. Unlike at Charlie Med, where I was dropped in like a hand grenade, I had been expected at China Beach. Captain Canada said that this would be the center of all neurosurgery for the navy and marines in Vietnam, and that made me nervous and more confident at the same time. As it turned out, for several months I was the only neurosurgeon in that part of Vietnam. I had an inkling of the magnitude of such a responsibility, but it really hadn't sunk in yet as I spoke with my new CO.

Captain Canada said that I would be provided with as much support as possible. This, he went on to say, would include an OR for all cases, a full military neurosurgical equipment set, and a corpsman assigned specifically to neurosurgery. He further specified that incoming head-injury cases would have priority for one of the four ORs equal to any chest, abdominal, or vascular case. He also advised me that China Beach would be able to hold postoperative patients for seven days.

With this mandate I proceeded to review the new surgical equipment assigned, and although it was not the best, it would get me through. I reviewed the corpsmen's backgrounds and experience and then chose one. He was eager to be selected and involved. Then the ORs were carefully inspected. The floors were concrete, and a real OR table adjacent to fair anesthesia equipment was positioned beneath bright overhead OR lights. No more operating in a crude field OR or on a wooden picnic table in a tent, leaking rain on my patient! No more flashlights for illumination of the injured brain! No more standing in inches of mud while operating! And no more using my imagination for anesthesia.

Following this I proceeded to the ICU Quonset and discussed the special needs of head-wound victims with the corpsmen and their supervisor, Tiny. He was about six foot three and weighed three hundred plus. Outgoing, motivated, and bright, he was a valuable asset to our soon-to-be-inundated ICU. My next contacts were the anesthesiologists. There were three, and after discussing the unique aspects of head-trauma surgery, I was confident they were equal to the task. They subsequently proved themselves scores of times.

Initially the hospital was assigned four orthopedists, four general surgeons, five or six internists, one neurosurgeon, three anesthesiologists, and approximately ten general medical officers. These were young physicians just out of internship who had not yet had specialty training in any branch of the wide spectrum of medicine. They were generally planning to pursue a specialty after their navy tour. Additionally, we had approximately eighty navy corpsmen functioning as nurses, operating room technicians, stretcher bearers, pharmacy assistants, and clerical assistants for medical administration. One surgeon was chief of surgery, and an internist was chief of medicine.

Those first days at China Beach were a whirlwind for me as I settled in and learned the routine. The war was heating up, marine troop volume was expanding rapidly, and we soon were hard at work trying to save lives. The casualty flow was sporadic, but when the choppers flew in we were flat out. Eighteen to twenty battle casualties within a period of thirty-five to forty minutes was not at all unusual, and the previously observed hiatus of fifteen to twenty-four hours with no incoming casualties was also not uncommon. This was a direct result of the intermittent marine "sweep and destroy operations" in the jungle.

I very soon realized that Captain Canada was a man of his word. He saw to it that I got whatever I needed, as long as it was available through a variety of official or unofficial channels. One of the several positive things things he did was grant me permission to assign nineteen-year-old Seaman Third Class Bart Bean as my immediate assistant, who turned out to be one of the best corpsmen at China Beach.

Bart was slight of build, weighing about 140 pounds. At only about five feet eight inches tall, he was rather lanky at that weight. When he walked, he did so with a bounce that bordered on a playful gait. This blended well with the look in his eyes, which was one of excitement, curiosity, and mischievousness. Bart was a studious-appearing young man who wore plastic-rimmed glasses, lending to him an air of intelligence. He had straight semi-black hair combed to the right. He possessed a most engaging personality and was exceedingly accommodating.

Bart was the son of a prominent professor of history at Ohio State University who had great hopes and expectations regarding his son's advanced education. Yet, after graduating from high school, Bart announced that he was joining the navy. His father, evidently, was not pleased.

Not to be dissuaded, Bart joined, and after going through "Corps School" (a multi-week training period for hospital corpsmen) at the naval hospital in San Diego, he was sent to Vietnam and to the G-4 hospital that subsequently became known as the Naval Support Activity Hospital, China Beach.

When I began working with him, it quickly became apparent that he was a hard kid to ruffle. He was never crude nor base. He was one individual totally insulated from the common human neurosis called anxiety. He could find an element of humor in practically any situation, and he often did, much to the great relief of the commonly felt unbearable tension. Yet, in doing so, he was not callous or abrasive. He would, in effect, design organization in the middle of chaos.

He quickly organized the necessary yet limited surgical instruments I required. If I needed a piece of equipment for surgery, I would describe what I needed and somehow within a day or so, something not too unlike just what I wanted appeared in the operating room for my use. If he could not steal it, he would make a deal with the Sea Bees and they would make it. What the terms of this manufacturing project were, I don't know and I never asked. It is my suspicion that what they wanted (liquor) he was able to commandeer through surreptitious means and somehow get away with it.

He operated in a casual yet deliberate and effective fashion. Whether his terms for favors from others were extra food swiped from the mess hall, a new pair of boots stolen from the supply Quonset, or the name of an attractive Vietnamese lady from Da Nang remains to this day a mystery.

Bart was not only intellectually and technically gifted. In addition, he had deep human sensitivity that he repeatedly demonstrated.

Of increasing concern in those chaotic early days at China Beach was the scarcity of some critical equipment and supplies. The problem was that getting what we needed from the United States through normal channels presented something of a logistical nightmare accompanied by an inevitable delay amounting to weeks at times. Ammunition, weapons, and food had top priority during those early months of the conflict. These were carried in by aircraft. Supply material lower on the priority scale traveled by ship from Oakland, California, to the Da Nang Harbor, a voyage of about 12,000 miles. This was at least a two-week trip.

More often than not I went to the supply officer with a request list. He was an amiable and willing agent who submitted forms routinely. One day, my anxiety mounting, I walked over to his Quonset and said, "My notion of a naval supply request is a scribbled note stuffed into an empty whiskey bottle and then thrown into the South China Sea." My anxiety vented, we both laughed. For me to stand patiently by and await nothing was frustrating. I needed rapidly depleting consumables while head-injury victims were carried in more and more frequently. Some would die if I didn't get help. These troops had trusted their lives to us.

One item was most important on the instrument table during a neurosurgeon's operation: "cottonoids." These are cotton strips a half inch wide and four inches long. They are critical in that they are used to line the margins of the exposed brain while operating in the central focus. They both suppress bleeding and protect exposed tissue from drying out beneath it. When I ran out completely, my corpsman, Bart, fashioned a reasonable substitute by stretching four-inch pieces of cotton and then pressing them under a hot metal plate. Not too bad! But they were a poor substitute for the real thing. I thought of the chief of neurosurgery at the Mayo Clinic and took the idea to Captain Canada. Thank God he was a humanitarian who placed human life above the navy's image by going outside the system to request equipment. He authorized a letter but said, "Keep it quiet. I don't want the American people thinking the navy cannot take care of its own." I promptly wrote the request, and its mailing was expedited. Gratifyingly three weeks later a box at least thirty inches on a side arrived, compliments of Mayo Clinic. In it was a note from the neurosurgery chief, stating, "Happy to help." It was full of at least two hundred packages of cottonoids, a two-month supply. We were back in business. A lot of troops profited by our newfound treasure. With time the normal navy supply mechanism functioned and the issue resolved.

Many of the supplies that made it to Da Nang were lost to pilferage and wholesale stealing by certain elements of the Vietnamese civilian population even though the navy did its best to limit this. It took place notwithstanding the security provided by the navy. To this end, there existed in Da Nang a well-dressed Vietnamese woman who drove the only Mercedes I ever saw in the country and who was commonly referred to as "The Dragon Lady." She operated the "Da Nang Mafia" and cavorted with many suspicious-looking cohorts. It was well-known that most of the stolen navy supplies ended up as her personal property, and it was also well-known that they were for sale to navy supply officers for a certain sum of American dollars.

On one occasion, we were running relatively low on both anesthetic gases and oxygen typically encased in the rigid large heavy steel pressure bottles that stand about four feet high. These pressurized canisters are of the utmost importance, of course, in any operating room. I recall one day seeing our supply officer counting a large roll of American dollars, placing it in a small metal box, and getting in a navy truck going to Da Nang. When he returned a few hours later, he had the necessary pressure canisters containing the all-important gases sporting the stenciled label "Property of US Navy," minus the money This lady was by all standards the local Mafioso in Southeast Asia.

What we physicians occasionally did at the individual (low-keyed) level was called "cumshaw," which in navy jargon refers to stealing from the right hand and putting it in the left. Such activity was of course beneath the table. The administrators functioned above board and were out of necessity spending American dollars to buy back supplies and equipment stolen from us. This might loosely be referred to as the chain of command. The process effectively maintained a reasonable inventory of vital supplies for China Beach while I remained on station. Sometimes we doctors had to pull a little cumshaw (frowned upon by the chain of command) to expedite a necessity. Such was often accomplished with the underground economy of the navy's chiefs. One of those times involved the untimely demise of our only working electrocautery machine.

An electrocautery is a critical piece of equipment consisting of an electrically charged probe that is used extensively to help control bleeding during surgery. The thing is mounted on a small rolling stand, is about fifteen inches square, and weighs about fifteen pounds. The sterile probe is connected to it by a cord roughly four feet long. Inside the box is a transformer that converts the incoming power supply via a wall outlet from low voltage and moderate amperage to extremely high voltage and minimal amperage so that when the tip of the probe touches the bleeding tissue of a patient, it will cause a spark, creating a heat lesion, and stop the bleeding. The patient's body then conducts the electrical charge back to the transformer in the electrocautery box.

In surgery there are a myriad of micro bleeding sites, in addition to the larger ones. Bleeding from the larger vessels is controlled with a tiny clamp called a "hemostat," or possibly with a ligature. But we needed the electrocautery to handle the multitude of bleeders from the smaller vessels. It is not possible to carry out modern-day neurosurgery without one. We had two in the compound.

One day, while in the middle of a cranial case, the unit I was using began to fail, although it still functioned at about 30 percent efficiency. I turned around and requested that one of the corpsmen go to one of the other operating rooms in the adjacent Quonset and see if he could borrow that electrocautery unit. Regrettably, the man who volunteered was a guy named Harvey, who was not the most intellectually gifted individual I have met. Len, my favorite anesthesiologist, a Texan with a thick Southern drawl, often said Harvey did "not have much hay in his loft."

Harvey, eager to help, rushed out the door at the end of the Quonset from my operating room, ran across the narrow wooden walkway connecting the two OR Quonsets, and grabbed the unused electrocautery unit, which was on a small cart with four rubber rollers. It rolled very well on the smooth concrete floors of the operating room in the Quonsets, but it didn't roll very well at all on the irregular slatted narrow walking deck connecting the two huts.

I was continuing to work when I heard a terrible crash. Harvey screamed, seemingly in agony. A few moments later, he came in looking like he'd been in a bar fight. He was covered with dust and sand and sported a bruised forehead, a skinned nose, and abraded hands and knuckles. He looked somber as he said, "The machine crashed, sir! I'm sorry, sir! The damn thing is wrecked."

Two of the other corpsmen rushed out to see and then returned. They confirmed that the machine had toppled over and been destroyed.

I swore under my breath, and I wondered what the hell we surgeons were going to do without a fully functioning electrocautery unit. We all wanted to strangle Harvey, even though he had meant well. For the next day or two, we struggled with a single malfunctioning electrocautery unit for all surgery at our hospital. We were well aware that to acquire a new unit through the standard supply lines would take many weeks, and we immediately dismissed that as a viable option. The only other unit was about twenty miles away at my old location, Charlie Med, but they needed it just as badly as we did.

Everyone at the hospital knew of our predicament. One the navy chiefs came up to me and said, "Doctor! I know the whereabouts of an electrocautery that is spotless and probably never gets used."

I was obviously stunned and disbelieving, however my ears perked up. I said, "Speak to me, Chief!"

The chief said, "Sir, on board one of the navy freight supply ships anchored in Da Nang Harbor, the ship's doctor maintains a small dispensary that includes, among other items, an immaculate electrocautery unit!"

Well, now we had part of the problem solved. We know there is a unit within striking distance, and we had the exact location triangulated. What remained was to get our hands on it and spirit it away from the owner and then into our hands. That prompted my next question. "Chief, what sort of deal can we strike with that doctor?"

He said, "Sir! My sources tell me that because he is confined to the ship as ship's company, he will never touch foot on Vietnamese soil, and he has an insatiable desire for a combat souvenir of the enemy, either one of their rifles, a knife, or a Viet Cong flag."

Well, the chief had me there. I wasn't in a position to obtain any of these items since I seldom got out of our hospital compound, and when I did, it was only into Da Nang, which was reasonably secure. Thus, I was quite unlikely to acquire any of these critical items. The chief then interjected that he had ways of obtaining the desired pieces of enemy goods. He stated that he needed my authorization to proceed.

I said, "Chief, that's quite patriotic of you," and then endorsed his clandestine plan, even though I had no authority whatsoever to do so. Within a few days, we had a shiny, spotless electrocautery unit with the typical riveted emblem on its case, stating, "Property USS 'Whatever.'" Our electrocautery problems were solved, and that instrument was jealously guarded, as if it were a newborn baby, for as long as I was at China Beach. The "Chief's Underworld" came through and definitely saved lives. I never did ask how the chief got the items from the Viet Cong. I frankly didn't really care.

So, no matter where we had to turn in the constant supply chase, we remained constantly vigilant to any potential source that could provide a solution to our problems. For instance, opportunity came along one late afternoon when a marine gunship was operating against the enemy not far from our facility, flying low while providing a close air support for the marines. Suddenly, the windshield of the craft was shattered by enemy small arms fire, and the ship lurched to the side as the pilot was struck in the head by a bullet. His copilot rapidly grabbed the controls, broke off the mission, and headed directly for our facility with his wounded comrade slumped in the cockpit. The helicopter landed, and the pilot was extracted from the damaged aircraft with some difficulty because of his location up forward in the craft securely held in place by the restraining belt.

Once he was successfully extricated, however, he was carried on a stretcher to the shock tent. I was called and quickly evaluated him. The round had entered slightly above his right eye and had exited near his right ear. He was semiconscious with no other injury in evidence. As in all these wounds, there was the familiar sight of blood and brain tissue emanating from both the wound directly above his right eye and the one near his right ear. Following the standard X-rays to confirm missile track, I was provided with surgical orientation. He was taken to surgery, where the necessary cranial operation was embarked upon. It went well.

After the operation, the victim was transferred to the intensive care unit and managed in the appropriate post–head-injury fashion. The next morning he was fully awake and not in significant discomfort. A marine captain, he was visited that following day by many of his fellow pilots, superior officers, and no less than a two-star marine general. His injury was not particularly unique when considered in the context of our head-injury patient mix. Ordinarily he would be evacuated to the United States. However, it happened that his wife was a navy nurse stationed in a US naval hospital in Japan; therefore, arrangements were made to evacuate him to that facility, as opposed to a naval hospital in the United States. It did not take long for my designing, self-serving mind to begin focusing on that naval hospital in Japan as a major source of additional supplies.

I shared my plan with the chief of surgery and the hospital commander, who concurred that we might strike "gold with respect to supplies." A few weeks later, the neurosurgeon at the naval hospital in Japan was temporarily transferred to our China Beach to replace me for a few days, during which period a flight was arranged to take me to Tokyo, ostensibly for a period of rest and recuperation. Far from it!

I flew to Tokyo all right but then made a beeline to the naval hospital about fifty miles outside of Tokyo. After arriving there, I presented myself to the hospital commander. He, having been advised that I would be visiting, expressed his gratitude for the care given to his nurse's husband and then asked if he could help me during my visit! I had no idea it would be so easy! I feigned hesitation and then mentioned that we sure could use a few things from his supply department. I then proceeded to outline our needs and was graciously shown the way to the supply office by the commanding officer himself, who said to the supply officer in charge, "Give him whatever he wants."

I felt like a child at a candy store with a $1,000 bill. I went up and down rows of equipment and medicinal supplies, stating to the supply officer, "I'll take three of these, and four of those, etc."

I do not believe he was very happy with my presence; however, he had to obey the order from his commander, and within a few days my bounty was crated and on a plane to Da Nang, where China Beach officials were waiting with a "Six-By" truck to claim the treasure.

In a sense I felt like a member of Robin Hood's band of thieves in Sherwood Forest—robbing from the wealthy lords and giving to the poor! Good old navy cumshaw! It was a good feeling. That day China Beach moderately enhanced its inventory of permanent and consumable supplies for the operation of the hospital.

Because of the increased US involvement in the war, our facility began to take more and more casualties. When I arrived in the country, there were about 200,000 American military personnel there, and when I left a year later, the number had swelled to 500,000, of which about 80,000 were marines.

The three marine facilities provided all medical care in north quarter Vietnam before China Beach became operational. As indicated earlier, there was just one neurosurgeon for all the marines and sailors. Marine hospitals are organic to the Marine Corps and staffed by navy doctors and China Beach was a naval hospital also staffed by navy doctors. Both types took care of marines. The marine hospitals were mobile, and we were fixed, going nowhere! The surgical capability of the China Beach facility was greater than that of the marine hospital where I was previously assigned by virtue of the fact that we were considered a permanent facility and, thus, were equipped with somewhat more elaborate surgical equipment, in addition to permanent operating rooms. Additionally, we had a more sophisticated intensive care unit, and just as importantly we were authorized to hold out patients seven days before evacuating them. Conversely, at the previous facility we were allowed to hold them just six hours. Here at China Beach, like the marine hospital, when evacuations did occur, they were picked up by helicopter from our landing zone in front of the shock Quonset and taken to the Da Nang airstrip about twelve miles away. From there, they were flown to Clark Air Force Base Hospital in the Philippines.

I gradually became accustomed to the surgical equipment, the operating room facilities, the new ICU, and the patient wards. Again, as at the previous hospital, the physicians would be notified that there were incoming casualties on board helicopters, and we then generally would migrate toward the shock Quonset to assist in triage of patients and to render emergency lifesaving care.

After evaluation we would advise the chief of surgery, who was always present of our individual priorities. He alone would make the decision as to which patient went to the operating room first. At that time at China Beach, in mid-March 1966, we had four functioning operating rooms, two in each of the two surgical Quonsets. As noted, the marine helicopter evacuation craft were instructed from headquarters near Da Nang that all head injuries should be conveyed to the China Beach facility. This order also extended to all naval ships along the coast and the South China Sea. Thus, my caseload continued to increase as the weeks progressed.

Accordingly, I was offered more support from the commanding officer with respect to corpsmen help and operating room time. I became quite familiar with my corpsmen. In time I grew to know and trust the anesthesiologists who were assigned to China Beach and the general medical officers who often were called upon to assist me at surgery. Time and time again, in came the groaning, twisting bodies, drowned out by the screeching helo engines. They came dirty, bloodstained, sometimes crawling with flies, limbs disfigured or gone, blood covered, mud impacted, scalp torn open like a tulip, and the egg white of brain tissue exposed and oozing. The orthopedists referred to this phenomenon as "the toothpaste syndrome." To the surgeons, such wounds represented a massive challenge, and to the uninformed they were nothing short of an unimaginable horror!

11

BLOODY SPRING

THE SPRING OFFENSIVES IN 1966 WERE nothing in comparison to those later in the Vietnam War, but for us at China Beach in those early days of the conflict the flood of wounded was so great we almost buckled under the constant pressure. At times, I felt like I lived in the OR, bathed in blood and brains, and breathed the vapor of death deep into my soul to the point of suffocation.

More than half of the marines on whom I operated had multiple traumatic injuries, usually from mines or hand grenades. That meant an entire team of surgeons had to operate on the soldier at the same time. It was common to see three to four physicians involved in a surgical procedure on one patient. These were in addition to the one anesthesiologist and the several corpsmen who passed instruments to us as our surgical technicians. Others ran in and out of the operating room for specific instruments, supplies, fluids, or blood.

One of the most memorable members of the medical staff in my early days at China Beach was a guy named Len, one of the initial three anesthesiologists assigned to the hospital. I came to greatly rely on him as I tried to save the lives of so many torn-up kids. Len was from Texas and had the typical dialect that so frequently echoed the connection to the state. He was of medium height, attractive-looking with a shock of blond hair that frequently fell over his right eye, necessitating that he often swept it up with his right hand, out of his line of vision. His skin was tan and ruddy-looking, and his eyes were blue and had a peculiar glint, a combination of seriousness and mischievousness about them.

He looked to me like the proverbial Texas Ranger, and he wore his sidearm like he was born with it. Beyond his physical attractiveness he had a gregarious and yet controlled manner that allowed him to come across as friendly and cooperative without being overbearing. Len never boasted of his medical expertise, nor was that necessary, for he was a superb anesthesiologist. Although he was characterized by a jesting manner, he possessed a deep side and was fully conversant with the lurking dangers of the region we called home. His temperament was never mercurial.

One day the marines were moving a relatively large contingent of troops into a potential heavy-combat engagement and requested a cadre of medical officers to move in convoy with them. This included an orthopedist, a surgeon, several corpsmen, and an anesthesiologist. Len was picked as the anesthesiologist, and that evening, although he was not a religious man, I saw him slipping quietly into the makeshift chapel for a "chat with his Maker."

Not only was I impressed with his ability to manage the hemodynamics and control the anesthesia of a badly injured patient during a complex operation, yet additionally his soothing personality was strikingly apparent during the several minutes while he prepared a patient for anesthesia. During this brief interval, many patients (sometimes including neurological cases) were awake and understandably frightened. Len characteristically would say to a young marine in a slow, drawn-out manner, "Where are you from, son?"

The young man, if he could, would usually echo his city or hometown, whereupon Len, in a seemingly surprised response, would say, "Well, how do you like that. I used to live in that town."

This gesture had a remarkably soothing emotional effect on many of these terrified, injured very young men. Len would then follow up very quickly by saying, "Do you remember the drugstore on the corner of—I can't remember the intersection of the streets—but it was down the street from a movie theater and not far from a hardware store?"

The patients, so scared yet eager to relate to someone from home, would believe in their own mind a locale with a drugstore, movie theater, and possibly a hardware store, and then say, "Yeah, yeah, hey, were you really there?"

At about this point, Len was beginning to inject intravenous anesthesia agents, and while babbling away in an almost happy mood, the young patients just dropped off to sleep. Len was clever enough to realize that this combination of buildings was present in just about every town in the nation. In the course of this deception, he conveyed tranquility to many young kids. Another very classic expression of his would take place as surgery was under way. I would frequently say, "Len? How's he doing?"

His response was always the same: "I won't hurt him if you don't!"

An additional Texas expression of his was his comment during the monsoon rains. He often said, "It's wetter around here than a cow pissin' on a flat rock."

I suspect that I did at least one hundred operations

with this man on patients whose conditions were often so critical that I wondered if we would ever get them out of the operating room alive. But he could do it!

Despite all the medical and malfunction adversities, including blood loss, macerated viscera, and massive head injuries, he never once lost control of a situation from the anesthetic perspective. Thanks to Len, many patients escaped from returning to the United States in body bags.

The amount of blood we used that spring was staggering, but a steady supply flowed to us from the frozen-blood storage facilities back in the United States under the administration of the US Department of Defense. Thousands and thousands of small plastic containers filled with donated blood lined the freezers. Once the blood was drawn, it was then processed in such a fashion that the serum was subtracted away from the red blood cells. Following this, the cells were bathed in a glycerol solution that did not expand like ordinary water when frozen, allowing the blood to then be frozen and stored without ruining the cells. Those small plastic bags could be stored for years. In the event of war they were thawed and used for casualty care.

Rivers of thawed blood came from our frozen-blood processing facility, which was housed in an olive-drab semitrailer, with its wheels half-sunk in the sand. It was parked next to the ORs for easy and quick access. The physician in charge of the blood was Jerry Long, a relatively small man about thirty years old. Like most of us, he had recently completed his training. He had blond, prematurely thinning hair, light-blue eyes, and regular features. When he spoke (and he did a lot of that), it was with a rapid delivery to the point where he lost control of the sentence sequence and stuttered a bit.

During months of tumult and give-and-take of field combat surgery, many doctors (including me) became irritated with enlisted corpsmen who worked under us. Jerry never once became agitated or irascible. I marveled at this personal control, and I envied him.

We were busier than ever in March, and the steady flow of casualties clearly helped me hone my skills as a neurosurgeon. I gained capability and confidence in dealing with major trauma management. Simultaneously, I became faster and faster executing the operative procedures. This confidence was bolstered by the results that continued to improve in terms of reduced mortality and residual disability over time. My initial draconian sensitivities gradually gave way to a robust, tangible sense of eagerness and a desire to work more and more. I was truly beginning to respect my ability as a neurosurgeon and relished my crucial role at the hospital. Coupled with my enhanced skill came a desire to do more and more in surgery to prove to any and all I was equal to the mission with which I was charged. This, in effect, was suppressing the guilt and insecurity I carried in my mental seabag on my journey to Vietnam. Obvious to me at this point was the fact that I harbored a need to be needed. It was being satisfied repeatedly now.

Indeed, this need manifested itself in many ways. In one instance, a marine platoon had just returned from a sweep-and-destroy mission, and the men were busy cleaning their rifles, when unfortunately one weapon still had a round lodged in it. In the course of cleaning it, it discharged. One man was struck in the chest, following which the high-power bullet passed into the head of a second man. He was brought to us promptly via Huey. I examined him and reviewed his skull X-ray and then walked up to his stretcher still in the shock Quonset. The location of the bullet was in an accessible part of his brain, and luckily he was still conscious.

"Private," I said, "you have a bullet in your brain, and I need to take it out in surgery."

His eyes opened wide in surprise as he said, "Have you ever done this before, sir?"

I was taken aback a bit, but before I could respond, the attending corpsman barked, "No, Private, but he has always wanted to try! Now hold still!"

Obviously, the marine did not take this well, but he was soon put under anesthesia in the OR. The surgery went well. Seven days later he was put on a plane to the United States, awake and happy to be going home. Unfortunately, not every case ended like that, which did not surprise me. However, even some of the most severe ones were not beyond saving through medical science. But along with saving the lives came some painful philosophical questions that to this day I still have not sufficiently answered to my own satisfaction. I think perhaps that's the case, because no clear and easy answers exist. The following is an example.

On a grueling spring day, I was called to the shock Quonset after a helicopter had landed, carrying yet another wounded marine. His flak jacket was blown apart, and his uniform was torn in many places. Blood was splattered over the limbs, chest, and face. The patient was still writhing in an agitated, confused state. It was a policy of the shock tent corpsmen to cut the uniform completely off the patient so that all parts of the body could be inspected promptly.

This particular patient had unfortunately been in the vicinity of an exploding device, probably a land mine, and had sustained multiple penetrations of his pelvis, arms, abdomen, chest, face, and brain. In addition, both legs were blown away at the mid-calf level, the right arm was splintered at the mid-upper arm level, and both eyes had been penetrated by missile fragments, rendering the patient completely blind. We promptly took him to surgery for management of the penetrating wound of his brain, abdomen, and chest, and for his shattered limbs.

The mood in surgery was more somber than usual for a reason most obvious to all of us. Finally, one of the anesthesiologists wondered out loud what kind of an existence this young man would have if he survived and went back to the United States.

We speculated that he would end up in a Veteran Administration Hospital for an extended length of time. Following this period of rehabilitation, we conjectured whether it was possible for his family to care for him in this profound state of disability. This was one of the few times that I almost hoped that my patient would not survive the surgery. He developed no complications in the seven days we were able to maintain him at our facility, however, and I remember watching him being loaded by stretcher bearers into the side port of a helicopter on the landing pad. It then lifted straight up and moved rapidly off toward the Da Nang Air Base.

I have no doubt that, after he completed rehab, he languished in his parents' home somewhere in America and cursed the doctors in Vietnam who had kept him alive. I had long since come to grips with standing aside and letting a patient die who I knew no one could save. This was different. I was not prepared to doom a profoundly compromised trooper I knew would survive if given assistance. It was and is a philosophical quandary, to be sure, but it was not up to me to play God in his case. Though I did play God in other situations.

Another patient, not one of mine, apparently had stepped on a land mine. When he arrived by helicopter at our facility, his uniform and gear were quickly stripped away. He had lost both his legs from a point about three inches below his hips on each side. He also had multiple penetrating wounds in both forearms and upper arms. There was surprisingly little involvement in the chest or abdomen and only a few small facial penetrations. He had no involvement of his brain. This patient represented a massive blood-volume management problem for the general surgeons over the next few days. Our final count was ninety-two units of blood to sustain his blood pressure and volume. Such was required to offset the amount of blood and serum lost through this high bilateral lower limb traumatic amputation. Amazingly his condition came under control, and we watched days later as he too, on a stretcher, was loaded on a helicopter, fully alert and talking, destined for Da Nang and then the United States. All of us shared a collective sense of accomplishment that this patient had overcome massive odds and was going home. Though he had no legs, he did have two arms, normal mental function, and of course, eyes, ears, and voice, all intact. But he would always be a cripple. I had mixed feelings about him, as well, though I had even more about the patient I described previously.

About three or four weeks went by, during which time we remained immersed in continuous surgical endeavors, when somehow a copy of the military newspaper called *Stars and Stripes* made its way to our hospital. This is the official newspaper of the US Armed Forces distributed worldwide. In a combat zone, it was not regularly delivered; however, this particular issue somehow made it to us. There was a full-page picture on the front showing the young marine we had worked on being assisted off an air force plane in Honolulu while his wife, who had apparently been brought out to Honolulu for the occasion, could be seen rushing across the tarmac to meet him. All of us studied the picture, and, for a moment, the collective depression and exhaustion prompted by the carnage of the war was lifted. I had to wonder, though, whether the couple's marriage lasted. I had to wonder if the man was able to find happiness in life. I will never know, of course.

Another night the familiar pulsating, ever-increasing roar of helicopter engines was heard descending toward our landing pad. Like robots, we surgeons moved to the scene. Three or four helicopters actually came in sequentially, each rapidly offloading their three to four casualties. After the corpsmen had carried the casualties across the tarmac to the shock tent and laid them across the sawhorses, their trauma included the now-familiar multiple penetrating sites, partial and complete amputations of various limbs, and some crush injuries.

One victim stands out in my mental imagery to this day. As most of them, he was a young marine less than twenty-one years of age, lying there with his combat khaki-colored uniform, heavy jungle boots, flak vest, and helmet lying above his head on the stretcher. Soil and mud covered his boots, and much of his legs, hands, and arms. Additionally, mud mixed with spattered blood covered his flak vest across his chest and abdomen. A great deal of blood was on his shoulders, and as I looked up to inspect his face, I realized that he had been struck tangentially from the right by a high-caliber missile, probably on the order of a .30-caliber machine gun bullet at relatively close range.

Before me was a concave collection of bleeding tissue from just below the eyebrow level to his upper neck region. Gone were his eyes, nose, and mouth. There was nothing in front of his ears. He had no face! He was breathing at a rapid rate through the bloody tissue where his mouth had been. To be sure, there was no threat to his life. If we simply provided him with an airway, his heart and lung function would be normal. Blood loss and an airway to breath were the only issue. This we could do—and did correct.

Back in the United States, skin grafting would cover his

face cavity. The fact that he would have to live the rest of his life with a concave-covered feature that was once his face suggested to me an enormous emotional problem. He would be tattooed with this repulsive appearance throughout the many years he had yet to live. Again, did we really help him? Even now, years later, I think of him.

On another day that I recall as hot and clear, I was summoned to the shock tent, not by an incoming helicopter, but because three marines were brought in from a local firefight, in the back of a military truck known as a "Six-By." I assumed the truck had been somewhere near the hostile activity and was the first thing available to the navy corpsman. The marines driving the vehicle motioned for me to come out and look for myself.

I climbed up into the bed of the truck and found three marines lying and covered with mud and blood. The first two were clearly dead, revealing ashen and blood-spattered faces, eyes half to three-quarters open, staring blankly into the heavens. They were still in their combat uniforms and flak vests covered with blood and a dark muddy substance.

The third was lying on his side. When I rolled him on his back, I realized that the left side of his head above the level of his left eye had been cut cleanly away, exposing what was left of the left hemisphere of his brain. Remnants of the Dura Mater, which covers the brain, mixed with dried and drying blood settled into the bed of the truck, forming a red semi-clotted gelatin pool. Flies were crawling and swirling about his partly amputated brain. Needless to say, he also was dead.

I climbed out of the back of the vehicle, walked around to the front, and instructed the driver to take the victims across the tarmac helicopter landing pad to a tent facility bearing a sign over the screen door: "Decedent Affairs." I strongly doubt that any of the three victims had the slightest sense of pain before their lives were extinguished. I wondered if these young marines were better off than the ones I just described. I still wonder today, years later.

Depending on one's perspective, the nature of the injuries brought to us ranged from impressive to striking if one is to describe them from the standpoint of the surgeon, and to ghastly if described from the perspective of a layperson. I asked myself rhetorically, "How many ways might a human body be dissected traumatically?"

I also wondered how many young men physically lost their dignity while we the surgeons were emotionally losing ours. I say this because, with each succeeding devastating injury, the emotional impact on me lessened, and I assume it was that way with my peers, as well. The patients simply became curious anatomic abominations from the battlefield.

On the many nights I could not sleep, I couldn't help but revisit the question about whether I was harming some of these kids through the very act of saving them, like the one with grotesque facial wounds. Wasn't I actually assuring them a crippling emotional future? In many of these cases, their survival could be guaranteed by my surgical skills, but the man would be perceived as hideous to any and all members of society. Is this what I would want for myself? No! However I'd been trained to save lives, and the navy clearly insisted that I do everything I could for each victim. On occasions, I sent home vegetative patients, but they were totally unaware of what had happened to them. They were like infants, shielded from years of mental turmoil and anguish.

I remained unable to resolve my dilemma. I could not find the answers I wanted. I don't think any of us could, and we all lost a lot of sleep.

12

THE COMMANDER

THE WAR WENT ON, AND THE casualty flow continued in a dreary, unending stream. Fever and sickness, mostly malaria, significantly increased, and the trauma never stopped. With the influx of patients, additional physicians were added to our staff, including (and most importantly, from my perspective) two additional anesthesiologists.

Equipment was also arriving on a more regular basis, much to our great relief. Replacement surgical instruments, anesthesia equipment, nonsurgical medical supplies, and other goods and materials routinely consumed in a hospital came in. We also finally got administrative support equipment, like typewriters and file cabinets, for the increasing load of paperwork associated with the steadily spiraling patient load. Our daily patient population was about 250. These included the non-surgery patients suffering from dysentery, malaria, sprained joints, exhaustion, infections, and depression. The daily surgical cases ranged from approximately three to seventeen.

All of us were becoming more proficient with the

management of trauma, both in the operating room and on the ward. The various types of injuries continued to come on a sporadic basis, and, as previously noted, it was unusual for just one or two to arrive. Six to seven, or more, would show up at one time, following which there might be a quiet period of twenty-four hours or so. This irregular patient influx was a direct result of planned military offensive operations scheduled by the marine higher-ups in the jungle.

One day while going about my activities on the hospital compound, Captain Canada walked up to me and introduced me to a new member of the orthopedic staff, a middle-aged commander named William Winchester. He was fresh from Anchorage, Alaska. About forty-five years old and about five feet ten inches tall, he had a stocky build and gray hair trimmed short as a crew cut. When he spoke, I immediately noticed that he had an exceptionally gravelly voice. He stared directly at me with dark eyes that seemed to pierce my own and penetrate to the depths of my soul.

In that instance I recognized Dr. Winchester for an individual who was confident, strong of will, and who had a solid bearing. Also, he lacked any semblance of humor. This was a person with a mind of iron and a personality of steel. We had a chance to walk over to a shady site and sit down, and I saw that he walked with a distinct limp to the left. I learned later of his phenomenal background, and I wondered why a man who had given so much to his country already had made his way back into a combat medical setting.

In the early months of WWII during the Guadalcanal Campaign, the navy operated a relatively small contingent of fast small-motor torpedo boats designated "PT boats." The boats, manned by a crew of five to seven, carried torpedoes and two large-caliber machine guns mounted in turrets. The mission of these craft was to operate primarily after dark and interdict small-invasion craft carrying Japanese troops.

In addition, they would carry out hit-and-run assaults on enemy shore positions.

William Winchester commanded one of these craft and dutifully discharged his mission assignment night after night.

Late one night he was ordered to search for a sister boat that had been run down by a Japanese destroyer. Survivors were still in the water. The commander of this particular boat was the young John F. Kennedy. As the weeks and months passed, the boat damage and casualty figures among this unique fighting force mounted. While on a mission, Lieutenant Winchester's boat came under heavy fire and was destroyed. He and most of his crew were able to swim to a beach on a US-held island where his badly injured left leg was deemed a threat to his survival and was amputated in a small medical facility by a navy corpsman.

Bill Winchester was then evacuated to the United States and fitted with a prosthesis, underwent rehabilitation, and during the remainder of the war attended college at the University of Michigan. He graduated and then entered the University of Michigan Medical School. After graduation, the young doctor entered and completed an orthopedic residency, moved to Anchorage, Alaska, married, and raised seven children.

During our conversation, he stated that he had stayed in the Navy Reserve. With the eruption of the Vietnam War, there began to well up in him a desire to get back into the middle of the action. An individual who is an amputee obviously would require a significant waiver by the Bureau of Medicine at the highest level in the navy. Obviously, he got it.

After we talked for a while, his somewhat gruff manner prevailed, and he said, "I have things to take care of, Pitlyk."

He went off to take care of business, and I watched him go. The man impressed me largely because of his evident inner strength and his clear dedication to his country.

Bill was immediately absorbed into the orthopedic section that included trauma management, surgical procedures, and postoperative care. Commander Winchester was a presence at China Beach, and most of us liked serving with him. One day, he was going about his duties when he turned and looked directly into the eyes of a gray-haired and very senior enlisted corpsman. At that point, the two men immediately recognized each other. The corpsman was none other than the man who had been forced to amputate Dr. Winchester's leg twenty-four years earlier on a beach at Guadalcanal. It was a very moving moment for both of these middle-aged men, but Bill only gave in to his emotions for a short time. Then both men returned to their duties.

Commander Winchester was the age of our commanding officer and at least twelve to fifteen years older than other physicians on the compound. He functioned routinely in a business mind-set. Indeed, he demonstrated nearly expressionless personal interaction and seldom errored. I had thought that I was energetic, but Bill outdid me by far. It seemed as though he was always at the shock Quonset looking for more work. If not there, he could be found on the wards dealing with his postoperative patients, setting a rapid pace from rack to rack, usually thirty patients, followed by his assigned general medical officer and two or three corpsmen.

As one might surmise, there were many young marines who lost limbs and who languished in our hospital, waiting to be sent home. It was common and quite understandable that amputees would develop reactive depression. They would lie in their rack, staring at the top of the Quonset hut, wanting to be left alone. Most did not want to go home.

While I was making rounds, I noticed that Bill routinely sensed it when a marine was lost in depression. Bill's usual plan was to wait two to three days following the patient's amputation before making his move. That would give the young man the necessary time to absorb the shock of what had happened. Despair typically followed the shock, which was not surprising to any of us, especially not to Bill.

I'd become aware of the pattern, and so I paid extra attention to Bill on the third or fourth day following an amputation. On morning rounds, he would sequentially go from rack to rack along the parallel line by which they were arranged in patient wards. When he reached the rack of the depressed man, he would turn to a corpsman and say, "Hand me the chart of Private Smith."

The corpsman complied. Bill then lifted his amputated leg, slid the pant leg up, and then put his foot directly on the side of the patient's rack. He placed the chart on his prosthesis and began to write on the chart. Not a word! The patient would see the angled piece of well-worn knee-like metal protruding from the pant leg, and he would suddenly realize that this high-ranking doctor was also an amputee. The impact and the effect were instantaneous and dramatic.

Without saying a word, Commander Winchester would complete his notation on the chart, pull down his leg from the patient's rack, drop the pant leg, and move on to the next rack. I suspect that the sixty-second course of psychotherapy did more to rehabilitate these young amputees than any more sophisticated psychiatric consultative and therapeutic maneuver offered by the navy back in the States.

Other Winchester anecdotes come to mind. They reveal the true grit of the man. One night at about eleven o'clock the raid siren went off. An attack was imminent. The Viet Cong always preceded an overrun with a mortar barrage.

Following this, they would be expected to cut through the concertina wire and attack us. The physicians were advised that, if attacked, their obligation was to grab their personal weapons, rush from their quarters to the patients' wards, and defend the entrances. When the alarm siren went off, I was near my quarters.

I quickly grabbed my weapon and a cartridge belt and ran as fast as I could across the sand to one of the patients' wards. When I got within twenty yards of the building, I heard the now-familiar guttural, gravelly voice of Commander Winchester, shouting, "Where is Pitlyk? Hiding under his rack?" Fortunately, there was no assault.

One bright, very hot day during the dry season, the drone of helicopter engines close to the buildings and descending into our compound was heard. By now we simply instinctively moved toward the shock tent. Curiously, just one patient, a Vietnamese soldier, was carried off the helicopter and across the tarmac to the shock tent.

I entered the building, and there saw a group hovered around the single casualty, who was lying in a supine position on a stretcher, stretched across the sawhorses. The group included three or four hospital corpsmen, two corpsmen assigned to the evacuation helicopter, and one doctor, Commander Winchester, who usually was the first to get to the shock tent and routinely was in the middle of any casualty event, whether it required an orthopedist or not.

I walked up to the stretcher, looked down, and saw a variant of trauma that sent a chill down my spine. A young Vietnamese trooper, whose clothes had been cut away per policy, was wide awake and had no injury to limbs or his abdomen, nor was there evidence of head injury. His eyes were wide in utter terror.

Then I saw it! On the front of his chest, on the left side,

a long vertical subcutaneous tubular-like mass stuck out from the level of his clavicle. It had the appearance of a firm tubular-like tumor between his skin and his rib cage. I then looked at the upper end of the wound and observed protruding from it the unmistakable fins of a mortar round. I knew this weapon well. All of us knew that this man was harboring a live bomb in his chest.

We were able to obtain a chest X-ray by moving a portable X-ray unit over his chest and orienting the cathode ray from front to back through his chest. We then placed an X-ray film cassette on a small box on the floor just under the stretcher and beneath the chest region. Then we took an X-ray. A few minutes later the film developed and confirmed our suspicions. It was a live mortar round. Worse still, the ignition device in the front had already been driven about 50 percent of the way inward when it struck this soldier.

A device such as this, when exploding, creates an excavation of a few feet deep in the ground and can kill all within a radius of twenty-five to thirty-five feet. The helicopter crew corpsman advised us of the circumstances. Apparently the patient had been in a group of twelve infantrymen who were trying to assault an enemy machine gun nest on the summit of a small hill about four to five miles out in the bush. They were unable to approach the machine gun because of its firepower. They summoned a tank, which then acted as a shield. The tank began to creep up the hill while the infantrymen crept close behind, waiting for a chance to get close enough to assault the machine gun or, better still, let the tank annihilate it.

What they didn't know, however, was that an enemy mortar team was hiding directly behind the machine-gun nest and began to launch rounds toward the tank. One of them landed just behind and hit our patient directly in the chest, fracturing his clavicle and, thus, partially arming this bomb and then slipping down into his chest outside the ribs and under the skin. The patient was evacuated back down the hill, picked up by a Vietnamese helicopter, and taken to a local Vietnamese military hospital, where the terrified surgeons refused to treat him. The Vietnamese chopper crew members were baffled. They radioed a marine helo unit. Our people flew in and picked up the stunned patient and brought him to us.

Dr. Winchester studied the X-ray, looked at the patient, and then, in his own inimitable expression, stared straight in my face and asked, "Will you help me with this case?"

I swallowed hard and nodded. "Okay!" I said, sounding a lot more enthusiastic than I felt.

In truth, I was terrified. I'd seen what mortar rounds could do, and the gruesome results flitted through my mind as we made preparations to transfer the patient to one of our operating rooms, place him under anesthesia, and then dissect out this bomb by a method not yet clear in our minds. My only solace was that, if the round went off, I wouldn't know what hit me.

A few moments later, the chief of surgery arrived on the scene, became apprised of the situation, and advised Dr. Winchester and me that we were not going to touch this man. He then wisely contacted the demolition personnel from a marine facility in the near proximity. They arrived on the scene, studied the X-ray, and confirmed that the firing pin was indeed halfway driven in. They further advised us that the only way that the mortar round could safely be removed from this patient would be to extract it perpendicularly to its long axis, which meant excising the skin and subcutaneous tissue around the perimeter of the device and lifting the skin-encased bomb directly away from the patient.

Needless to say, this is not what Bill and I had in mind.

We had designed to make a smaller incision over the region and then pull the mortar along its long axis rather than perpendicular to it, sort of backing it out of the long wound track. Had we proceeded, we would have died instantly.

The chief of surgery told us, even though he was terrified, it actually was his responsibility to carry out the procedure, and his assistant would be a member of the demolition section. All personnel other than the chief of surgery, the demolition expert, and the anesthesiologist were ordered 150 yards from the OR. The operation took approximately one hour. Everything proceeded well, there was no explosion, and the soldier and his bomb were separated. He made an excellent recovery, thanks to the chief of surgery looking directly into the eyes of death.

All through the many months I worked so closely with Bill, I was never granted the honor of being referred to by my first name, "Doctor," or even "Lieutenant," nor did I refer to him by any title other than his rank, "Commander." Additionally, Commander Winchester never confided anything in me regarding his personal life following the day we met. Despite the seeming coldness toward me, I truly believe there was a hidden undercurrent of professional and personal respect. I sincerely hope that this is not just wishful thinking.

We continued to respond to incoming casualties and did our best day after day, night after night. It was often surreal at China Beach. We'd be rushing to save a life while the thud of artillery boomed in the distance, reminding us of the war and how our efforts in the OR seemed futile on more than one occasion. At night, just like at Charlie Med, flares were used to light up the area to scare off the Viet Cong, except that high-flying planes dropped aerial flares over the beach instead of marines firing them off at the edge of the jungle. Those flares painted the sky and our entire compound with a pale yellowish hue. Because of the nightly sky show, I very seldom observed and enjoyed the stars (my hobby).

As time wore on, many of my colleagues and friends began to rotate back to the United States after their year in-country came to an end. Physicians with comparable skills replaced them, so there was no interruption of continuity of care. I became aware that one doesn't always appreciate the closeness, friendship, and camaraderie that develops between people until they are forced to sever the relationship. I tried to prepare myself to say good-bye to several. This was difficult, for I was feeling abandoned. With every good-bye came a distinct sense of loneliness. Indeed, I felt creeping abandonment, be it not major, for I continued my duties and transitioned with new physician members of the staff.

In my mind, it was as if the original vanguard of physicians and corpsmen had come, established a strong hospital as a potent medical force in the region, and now were allowing it to degrade. This, of course, was an absurd conjecture on my part, for even though they had been the original providers, they certainly were not irreplaceable. The incoming personnel, both professional and support types, were also capable individuals.

I ranked in age among the older specialist physicians at China Beach. There also was another group that included slightly younger doctors who had completed internships but who had not gone into residencies. They might best be characterized as general practitioners. Their function was to works as assistants to the specialists in that they would help at surgery, help manage patients in the wards, and man the shock tent on a twenty-four-hour basis.

As it evolved, the group tended to focus their energies in one area rather than continue to rotate about. Thus, the shock tent physicians set up a rotation and did only that.

Others assisted at surgery and, of course, did just that. The remainder worked with the internists and managed nonsurgical patients via nonsurgical care.

Walter Bancroft was one of these support staff, and although he lacked sophistication and self-confidence, he was someone most everyone liked. He came from somewhere in the Southeast, and he had a distinct Southern dialect. He was a large man, probably six one or six two and weighing at least two hundred pounds. He had a somewhat broad head and light-brown hair and wore wire-rimmed glasses. The distance between eyes was diminished such that his eyes seemed somewhat closer together than one would expect for the average man.

Walter walked with a somewhat pigeon-toed gait and never seemed to be able to get his uniform on just right. It always appeared as if it had been slept in for three days, with his pants slightly drooping. His jungle boots were dusty, and his hat, which the military referred to as a "cover," was generally on crooked. It also appeared that it had been residing under a heavy container for weeks on end.

Walter was a kind person, not the least bit aggressive and never irritable. His most distinguishing characteristic, however, was his inimitable personal demeanor. His tone of voice was imploring, frequently apologizing for some personal misadventure and never at all offensive. Whatever the purpose of his duties and activities in the operating room, he made every effort at perfection, regrettably though usually setting the operation back by thirty minutes or so. What he lacked in self-confidence and dexterity, he made up for in determination to properly achieve any task given to him.

In many ways, Walter was a big adolescent boy—eager but clumsy, honest yet not thoroughly grounded in the reality of the situation.

Late one night, we were in the middle of surgery. As I recall, the patient required the involvement of an orthopedist and a general surgeon simultaneously, each of whom would have an assistant, in addition to me. On that night Walter was going to be the neurosurgical assistant. The anesthesiologist and the "circulating corpsman" were also included in this busy assemblage of humanity. Thus, there was congestion around the OR table. I was looking at a leg injury at the request of the orthopedist for the purpose of inspecting a possibly injured nerve, when Walter asked what he could do.

I said, "Walter, I would like you to thoroughly scrub around the patient's scalp to ensure that we are not missing a penetrating head injury hidden under all the dirt, debris, mud, and grease."

While I was inspecting and exposing the damaged nerve in the patient's leg, I was interrupted by Walter at the other end of the table, who noted that while irrigating around the ear region, white flecks of material were coming from the region of the ear.

Without bothering to look, I made the supposition that this was more debris. "Go ahead with the squirting. Don't stop until you get all that white grit out of his ear." He did so, but more white flecks of material emanated.

At some point, I finished what I was doing on the patient's left leg and moved up to the head of the operating table. Then I looked with amazement as I witnessed Walter irrigating forcefully into the right ear and ejecting small flecks of damaged brain material from the ear canal.

"What the hell are you doing? That's brain tissue going down the drain. This guy is going to need surgery to fix the leaking brain area."

Poor Walter was embarrassed and humiliated by what he concluded as his misadventure. "I'm sorry, Doctor, but I tried to tell you." He really felt that he was the reason this poor patient would undergo a craniotomy. I assured him it was not his fault. "We can fix this, so let's get to it."

I did (with Walter's anxiety-ridden assistance) carry out the necessary surgery and correct the problem, following which the patient did well.

Poor Walter's self-image was further damaged, however, in spite of additional efforts on my part to mitigate his anxiety. "You proved the presence of an injury that required surgery," I said repeatedly. His sense of defeatism, however, could not be squelched.

For the rest of our tour, Walter would continue to wander about, walking somewhat pigeon-toed, uniform in total disarray, and with his cover looking as if he had been sitting on it for weeks. His rimmed glasses were always slid slightly forward on his nose, and through them one could see his eyes and the pleading image they aroused in any observer. Needless to say, he was thoroughly accepted by all the physicians and corpsmen on the staff as he moved about, doing his best, speaking in his low monotone voice, and making every attempt to discharge his duties and obligations to patients and superiors alike.

Even now, many years later, I occasionally recall with amusement that large, bespectacled, sardonic-faced figure lumbering along with his totally nonmilitary appearance, working his way toward the operating room Quonset, where he would do his level best to assist in any way, no matter how rough things got.

13

BETWEEN DARKNESS AND LIGHT

THE END OF SPRING APPROACHED WITH the slow passing of May, but you really couldn't tell. The seasonal changes in Vietnam were far different from those of the Midwest. No spring tulips or crocuses sprouted in colorful gardens. Robins did not hunt for worms on the front lawn. The cold fingers of winter did not give way to blessed caressing warmth. It was all humidity, rain, sand, and more sand, and, of course, the endless parade of battered, torn, and shattered bodies that passed through China Beach as the war machine ground on and on and on.

At Charlie Med in the late fall and early winter, I'd been scared, overwhelmed, and unsure of my abilities as a neurosurgeon. I'd had good reason to worry, but with the amount of surgery I worked on, my experience and skill had grown to the point where I knew I was at least a capable neuro-trauma surgeon. I was ready for the next challenge, though the constant bloodbath did get to me once in a while. Curiously, or perhaps not so curiously, I had also noticed for quite some time that the grim condition of the marines who landed on my operating table was having less and less of an impact on me emotionally. Looking back on it, I guess it was natural for me to become numb to the human tragedy playing out before me almost every day.

The lack of compassion I developed for the suffering of others was becoming more apparent. Then I remembered the comment from one of my teachers at the Mayo Clinic. "A neurosurgeon must have the heart of a lion and the touch of a woman." I tried to separate emotions from reality, sometimes perceiving myself as walking over mangled bodies of shattered marines without so much as bothering to look down. Clearly I was desensitized. Another noticeable change in my mental posture was the total subsidence of any element of personal fear.

At this stage of my tour, I frequently thought about the overly magnified sense of personal fear I had suffered while flying into Saigon on the Air Transport Command C141 and also on the air force freight plane ride up from Saigon to Da Nang—both well-recorded personal observations! How come I was negating fear in this hostile environment? I didn't know then, but now years later in a retrospective state, it's less opaque to me. I was simply adapting to a dangerous environment, a function of my limbic system.

A typical example of this mental process we humans are endowed with is evidenced by the following example. One day I had a chance to speak to a friend who was a crew chief on board a medium-sized marine helicopter called a CH-46. This craft was considerably bigger than the UH-1s to which I was accustomed. Its job was to deliver groups of troops into a combat area referred to as a "hot zone" and then get away while evading fierce enemy fire. My friend told me of his overwhelming fear in the first several missions, each of which were replete with enormous personal risk.

"After twenty or twenty-five missions, I just didn't give a damn anymore," he said.

I knew him relatively well and do not think that this was the remark of a depressed or maladjusted man. Rather, it is evidence that the human emotion—more specifically, the emotional part of the brain—has the capacity to make adjustments necessary to function in most environments in which an individual becomes immersed. I also have seen this many times in my private practice after the navy. It was particularly noticeable in patients who sustain spinal cord injuries. They become instantly paralyzed (either legs or arms and legs). For a period of time they are all depressed; however, in a matter of months they make an adjustment. Were it not for this capacity, it is quite possible that we would not accommodate and function under stress, whether it be physical (loss of a limb or blindness) or emotional (loss of a loved one, divorce, financial ruin). Most of us would then mentally decompensate and fail to respond responsibly to any threatening challenge, be it large or small. I am of the belief that this is a gift from evolution, as defined by Darwin. Should we not have the potential to call upon this impressive mental capacity, then we might hesitate to meet and accept challenges in life, thus settling for much less—hardly a thrust toward social progress.

Barraged with numerous and complicated battle casualties, we frequently would bring to a successful resolution one multi-injury casualty, including postoperative care, when another equally massively injured individual would appear. Both physical and emotional fatigue took their toll on corpsmen and medical officers alike. At times, it seemed that it would never end. This endless fatigue tended to spur loneliness. We all felt it, but of course loneliness is such a personal thing. The married men felt it more profoundly than I did.

Spring gave way to summer, and the dog days of August seemed to exaggerate the dreary monotony of our surroundings. Along with the weather, the war had continued to heat up by the middle of 1966, and our caseload likewise increased, exacerbating the emotional ups and downs, and the equally pervading sense of numbness. It was an odd place to be from an emotional and psychological perspective, a sort of yin and yang of the soul. The compound, with its sand dunes and dark Quonset huts, the concertina wire and guards closing us in, the heat waves dancing in the thick semi-humid air—it all combined to imprison us in a weird netherworld of incredible emotion that ran the gamut from joy to utter despair.

After long hours at work, all that you could look forward to was walking two hundred yards or so to your Quonset and its dubious comforts. The only escape was the nearby officers' club. It had a good supply of liquor and the promise of some more interesting and pleasant conversation than was to be had in the OR or the ICU. These conversations and discussions among the physicians and the Medical Service Corps officers frequently carried late into the evening, and they were a balm to most of us, I'm sure.

I also liked to be alone in the officers' club late at night, with the place all or nearly to myself. I was listening to tapes of Barbra Streisand while I sat there with my feet up on a chair having a drink at two, three, or four o'clock in the morning. Why I enjoyed listening to that performer so much (I had not even heard of her before I went to Vietnam), I don't know. Furthermore, I have not listened to her more than three times since returning home decades ago. Who knows why? The passion in her voice and her singing clearly bolstered my spirits and my ability to endure.

And then there were people like Smitty, as everyone called him, who seemed to calm the stormy waters merely with his presence. Smitty was the officer in charge of the pharmacy Quonset, and he ran it like his own quiet little kingdom set apart from the frenetic insanity that went on just outside his domain. He was middle-aged with crew-cut red hair and was always quick to smile even when I'm sure he didn't feel like it.

After a long day and possibly night of surgery, at about nine or ten in the morning, I got into the habit of reviewing X-rays from the day before. These were located in the X-ray Quonset near the ORs and the pharmacy. If I could, I'd take a detour next door to pay a visit to Smitty, which always rejuvenated me, often more than just a little. Though he was not a physician, he was vital to the ongoing operation of our busy hospital, in that he was responsible for the acquisition and dispensing of all drugs and medications necessary for the treatment of our patients.

Smitty efficiently and effectively acquired through the chain of command the appropriate medicinal supplies when the hospital began operation, and he ensured during his entire tour that as supplies were consumed (often at a phenomenal rate), replacements were constantly brought on board, such that in the many months I spent at the facility we never once ran low on any particular drug. His devotion to duty and professional performance was not the only reason he was revered. Smitty had a human side that was the envy of many of us. His outgoing, amiable, accommodating manner was constantly on display for all to absorb and relish. In no way was he self-absorbed.

In our charged and not uncommonly chaotic emotional environment, he was remarkable for the fact that he could maintain a balanced temperament (pouring water on the flames) plus a lighthearted and an enthusiastically helpful demeanor. Our visits would start out with my sauntering up to the counter, where he would be working on some thing or another, and nearby would be his ubiquitous coffeepot that exuded a pleasant fragrance of coffee that drew the doctors like moths to lamplight. A couple of pharmacy technologists were always busily moving among the various shelves containing different pharmaceuticals. In their immaculate uniforms they were efficiently filling prescriptions and requests from various parts of the hospital.

I always had the sense when walking into his Quonset that everything was under complete control. The corpsmen moved almost silently in this discharge of their duties, and seldom could you hear him directing them to the location of a particular drug or dosage as required. Smitty was never interrupted to clarify the interpretation of a requisition. One just knew they had been thoroughly trained and that they deeply respected their leader. His place ran as smoothly as the Mayo Clinic.

"Why, good morning, Lieutenant Pitlyk!" Smitty would say. "How are things in the OR?"

"Rough one last night, Smitty," I'd say, or words to that effect.

"Well, what can I do for you, Doctor?"

"I'd love a cuppa Joe," I'd say.

Smitty was happy to oblige. He would project the feeling that he had nothing to do but chat with me and the rest of the staff. I never heard him make a critical remark of another physician, Medical Service Corps officer, corpsman, or patient. His remarks and candor were always cheerful and connoted eagerness to be of assistance. Believe me, there was ample reason for open criticism toward various personnel including me.

The restricted, confined environment of the hospital, coupled with the enormity of the patient load, associated complications, and mounting emotional stress, tested the very fiber and mental resolve of each and all of us.

For me, walking into his clean, brightly painted, quiet pharmacy and seeing him standing on the other side of the counter next to the coffeepot, with its fresh aroma of brewing coffee, ready to offer a greeting, was in many ways a form of psychotherapy—or "a touch of home." To say his place was an oasis of calm in a sea of madness would not be overly dramatic. It was as if I was stepping out from under an umbrella of turmoil, confusion, hostility, frustration, and aggression to sit down in a fireside atmosphere, his home. When visiting, one walked into a serene, tranquil, accommodating, and supportive envelope, all this the innate invention of Smitty.

He might open up the conversation by telling me that he had received a letter from his wife back in San Diego and that all was going well. He would then immediately shift the conversation from himself and ask if I had heard from my family. He would inquire about what it was like when I was growing up, my friends, my family, my early schooling, my brothers and sisters, and even my pets. This man could lift me from Vietnam and its turmoil to another level of existence. During such, I could discuss (and he would eagerly listen to) my ravings about my plans after Vietnam, family, girlfriends, and career ideas. Whatever had bombarded me in the previous day I could unload on him. Patient load, acrimony, or an untoward bad result following surgery seemed to vaporize, and anxiety was suppressed and replaced with at least the illusions of tranquility.

This man represented in many ways a parental image to me, and I suspect he did so to many of the other younger physicians. This is not to imply that I did not have a father-son relationship with my real father; rather, I am suggesting that he in a vicarious way filled the void some 14,000 miles from my own father.

Another of Smitty's responsibilities was that of

"entertainment officer." This primarily involved obtaining as often as possible a movie to be shown in the officers' club at about eight o'clock each night.

The movies themselves were generally old, in black and white, and were seldom of Academy Award caliber. However, they truly were morale enhancing. The reels themselves had been passed from base to base and from ship to shore so many times that they were well worn and frequently broke two or three times during a run.

The characteristic sudden bright-white screen, loss of sound, and *flip, flip, flip* of the frayed end of the film on the spinning reel triggered loud shouts of obscenities, accusations of sabotage, coupled with "Hang the projectionist." Since Smitty was operating the projection equipment, he was the target of these strong albeit collegial verbal blasts. He cleverly reacted to the barrage of remarks each time the reel broke or the sound went off, or the power failed, or the artillery fire in the background overwhelmed the sound track in the film. He might then make such cavalier remarks as "The navy does not pay me enough to run this damn thing," or "I lost the directions on how to operate the projector," or "My wife never tolerated movies back in San Diego," or finally, "How do you expect me to do a good job as projectionist when I am busy drinking martinis?"

Smitty also had the ability to quell, by ever-so-subtle means, friction that occasionally developed between individuals, be they physicians, Medical Service Corps officers, or corpsmen. Smitty saw good and value in everyone on the base and made that clear by his expression, attitude, and genteel nature. Later, when I returned home, I saw him a couple of times, and we enjoyed catching up on what each of us was doing.

With the constant and clearly unrelenting surgical caseload, including the complicated postoperative management occurring day after day, I often lost count of the difference between Tuesday and Sunday, and after a while I didn't care. This, in concert with the broiling heat and the nagging thought of an enemy overrun on any given night, occasionally caused me to wonder why I did this to myself. We were frequently advised by marine security to be constantly conscious of the chance of an overrun. To this end we kept a loaded rifle in each operating room and dug and maintained a foxhole next to our housing Quonset and another one adjacent to each of the ORs. We also avoided venturing close to the concertina fence surrounding us and, after dark, traveled between our bunks and the patient-care area via a security jeep.

I had given up personal and professional friendships and a budding practice back home. I'd given up my girlfriend, Alice, and a brand-new convertible. This was, as I viewed it, an avocation! The seemingly constant insults to our emotional network (or, more technically speaking, the emotional part of the brain) were something that was characteristically not discussed among ourselves. I suspect the underlying rule of adhering to the Anglo Saxon male ego—suppress and ignore emotional stress and negate feelings—was no doubt a major factor in this collective attitude of our physicians.

Naturally, attempting to do work under trying circumstances did create a great deal of personal stress. It was nicely deflected though by some notion of achievement. This was an environment where one did not go to his home at night for solace, refuge, and emotional support by loved ones. Rather, we routinely interacted with each other day after day, ignoring our emotional needs. We then turned our emotional energy away by denying our personal situation or speculating what it would be like when it was over. I did realize, however, that everybody must feel pretty much like me. Thus, I was not alone in this truly silent "group therapy."

Though I'm not a psychiatrist, this I think was valuable mental therapy.

There were other kinds of therapy too. On occasion, an entertainer or celebrity would come to Vietnam to entertain the troops and make an effort to come to the hospitals. They would often be brought to the Da Nang airfield by helicopter during the daytime, meet the injured, put on some sort of entertainment program, and then be taken before dark by helicopter back to the airstrip and then out of the country.

One day I was going about my activities on the hospital wards when in came a helicopter, and out of the side door came a beautiful, long-haired, blonde woman wearing a light-blue formal dress and looking as radiant and attractive as any movie star I had ever seen. She was a singer from Australia. Her voice was good, and her appearance was phenomenal.

She walked through the patient Quonsets between the rows and racks of injured marines. She moved up and down the center aisle, singing and smiling, yet all of us knew well that if she didn't sing a note or say a word, she would easily achieve her objective. Not only had the wounded been totally mesmerized by her stunning beauty, but even the medical staff (including me) were most impressed by this image of Venus. None of us had seen a Caucasian woman in many, many months; however, even if we had, most would have still been transfixed by this striking young singer.

She arrived in the midafternoon and continued to spend time with the wounded troops, both singing and dallying at the side of bunks here and there, often talking individually with the men. She stayed on quite late in the afternoon and, even after the sun went down, was still entertaining and engaging in conversation. At this point, it was decided by the security force that a night movement out of the area was not entirely safe. She was invited to eat dinner with us, which she agreed to. During this time, all of us had a chance to meet her and savor the moment.

The commanding officer arranged, via the marine security forces, for the hospital to use one end of a Quonset somewhere near the center of the compound, which functioned as a storage facility, as an overnight lodging site for the young woman. A bunk was moved inside the building, and a small bedside stand and even a chair were provided.

Finally, after nightfall, dinner, and all of us having had a chance to talk to her, she was escorted to her Quonset, and a marine armed guard was placed outside the door at either end of the structure. All seemed safe and secure.

About two hours later, we heard a bloodcurdling scream coming from the direction of her sleeping quarters. Marine security rushed to the site and found two pajama-clad young ambulatory patients limping and scrambling up the side of the Quonset, trying to enter one of the small windows. Indeed, she had impressed the wounded marines enough to reclaim their manly instincts.

After the interlopers were hustled away for a night of "watchful care," two additional marine guards were placed on either side of the Quonset to ensure that no more midnight folly would be attempted.

The following day a helicopter was brought in to take her off to her next point of entertainment. After she had awakened and been provided with the use of the officers' shower under a highly secure arrangement, she now presented herself in a yellow formal dress, looking even more radiant than the day before.

She scurried across the sand, waved good-bye, and hopped into the helicopter to be taken elsewhere to continue her tour. It was many days before even the medical staff stopped talking about the "Australian singer." There were a few male movie stars and popular figures in the United States who came and offered moral support. Without a doubt, however, she represented one of the most tangible aspects of moral support that I was witness to in my time there.

But the moments of levity were few and far between. The reality of China Beach was by necessity grim because we were at war and our soldiers were being killed and wounded. It was our job to patch the kids up when we could and to give them comfort when we couldn't.

One morning the marines had begun an assault from the sea about fifteen miles south of us, and we all knew we'd soon hear the roar of choppers on the landing pad. Sure enough, the casualties began to come in shortly after the fighting started. During the landings, an unlucky marine ran out of the bow door of an amphibious tractor, but a Viet Cong sniper shot him before he had gone five feet. The bullet struck him just below his head. He fell to the ground, paralyzed and unable to breathe, and yet he was fully awake. The accompanying corpsman rushed to his side and gave him mouth-to-mouth, and another corpsman joined in the effort to breathe for the man while he was medevaced to China Beach.

I examined his wounds and recognized that he was unable to move his legs or arms. We obtained X-rays of the cervical regions and on the films could identify small metallic fragments radiating along a straight line from the entrance wound just below his jaw on the right, and exiting just behind and below his left ear. The condition was quite obvious. I confirmed the fact that the bullet had severed his spinal cord just below the brain level, thus interrupting the patient's ability either to perceive sensation anywhere from the neck downward or, worse still, to move any muscle from the shoulders downward, including the diaphragm (or the muscle used to breathe). No surgical, medical, or rehabilitation treatment could help.

Even more disturbing is the fact that all such patients are fully alert. Fortunately, they are nearly pain-free. Within a short period of time, however, they recognize how compromised they are. They can see, hear, and are fully aware of their environment. This type of injury is devastating. Such a victim is completely and permanently incapable of moving even a single finger. Uniformly, patients such as this are committed to a mechanical ventilator if they are to survive. Usually they do not.

It was apparent that this young man recognized his plight, for he lay there, in his blood-spattered partly cut-away uniform with helmet and flak jacket on the floor next to his stretcher, unable to speak. His wide eyes opened with a piercing, pleading stare, connoting to me his intense anxiety and fear. I tried to comfort him with optimistic words. I then said in a chuckling voice that he was lucky in that he was going to be going back to the United States quite soon, again trying to make him feel better, even though I knew it was futile.

I had him transferred to the intensive care Quonset hut, on the ventilator, and wrote orders for a tranquilizer agent to offset his anxiety, and antibiotics to help prevent lung infections and bladder infections I knew were not far off. After assuring myself that he had all that could be offered from any doctor, I walked back to my quarters.

As I wandered across the sand and gravel the short distance to my bunk, this young man's entire future burned into my mind. Literally, he had no future. I wondered why nothing could be offered to him. I was sure the corpsman thought he would do well—so many times they had seen injuries to marines that ostensibly looked severe; however, following surgery many of these patients improved and actually recovered. After all, this body had only a single, tiny wound of entrance just below his jaw on the right and another one just below his ear on the left, which did not appear ominous to the uninformed eye.

There were two big things that corroded the emotional fiber of a surgeon like me. One was to carry out an operation and make the patient worse, and the other was to be forced to turn your back on a patient who desperately was crying for help. Knowing you could do nothing was terrible, though there was another part of my mind that said he'd be better off if he died. I had been victimized by both of those seeming conflicting concepts in my brief career as a fledgling neurosurgeon in Vietnam. However, for reasons that I was unable to fathom at the time, this particular event plunged me into a transient state of depression. Mercifully, the Angel of Death came to this young man's aid. Two days later he died.

That night, things were quiet so I walked out of my Quonset and climbed up on top of the officers' club Quonset adjacent to my living quarters, on the flat wood platform that we (the doctors) built on top of the Quonset. It connected by a crude ladder-like stair from the sand up to this slightly elevated oasis. We had some wicker chairs of a sort up there, and this platform was frequently used by the medical staff for emotional escape. It also provided for us an overlook of the compound. We could see the fifty or so Quonset huts appearing like deep gray-colored groundhogs crouching on the sand. The security forces advised us that it was unwise to go up there since it represented potential exposure for snipers who might be beyond the limits of the compound, hiding in the wooded area.

Initially that risk bothered me and others; however, curiously as time passed, our fear translated into complacency, and many of us climbed up there to sit and think, to wish or hope, possibly to get away from it all. In an odd way, it was "eons" away from the compound. On this particular night I was disturbed over the young marine's death as I sat down in one of the little chairs on the wooden platform and stared into the flare-speckled night sky.

The ever-present aerial flares descending slowly to the ground in small parachutes were back right on schedule. After bursting into brilliant light, they projected a yellowish glare, which, along with many other slowly descending flares, bathed the hospital compound in its strange light. As they got closer to the ground, they cast longer and longer shadows across the terrain. The Quonsets looked again like immobile rodents hiding on the surface of the sand, entirely motionless. In the distance one could hear the continuous thundering roar of outgoing rounds from marine howitzers. This night, the moon was full, and the sky was cloudless, though the stars were obscured by the brilliance of the flares. I wrote a letter home, and although I don't remember the nature of the letter's context, what I do recall so well was that the moon was of such brilliance, I did not need a flashlight.

In time, the moon got tired and I did too. It slipped beyond the hills to sleep, and I descended down the ladder and went to bed. I lay staring for some time into the face of that terror-stricken marine, to whom I could offer only abandonment, and then slipped into a troubled sleep.

14
NOBLE ATTEMPTS

PRIOR TO ARRIVING IN VIETNAM, I was advised by the Bureau of Medicine in the navy that my mission might not be entirely restricted to neurosurgery. Indeed, depending upon the magnitude of casualty flow, it might be necessary to assist general surgeons in abdominal, thoracic, or vascular surgery. Most of the time, however, my service was not required, and I was thus able to restrict activities to that relating to neurosurgery. It was my perception that the surgeons were so relieved to have someone take head injuries, specifically the nuances implied in their care, off their hands that they avoided bothering me with other matters.

On one occasion, however, a marine had sustained a gunshot wound through the neck, entering just to the left of the midline, where his trachea, which is more commonly called the windpipe, is located. It then passed through and exited his back just to the right of the spinal cord. There was no involvement of the spinal cord and, therefore, no neurosurgical consideration. The patient was bleeding rapidly, however, from the wound of entrance just below the mandible on the left side. On inspection it became evident to any surgeon that the bleeding was arterial rather than venous and would require immediate surgical attention if the patient's life was going to be salvaged.

Fortunately during my training I had experience with vascular surgery and, more specifically, the carotid artery, which was the artery damaged and leaking blood so profusely. Thus, I knew the anatomic relationships in the area rather well.

The general surgeon asked me to assist him, and the patient was taken to the operating room, where he was placed under general anesthesia by the anesthesiologist. The bleeding site, which was literally pumping blood in a pulsatile fashion much like a small water spout, was cleansed by a corpsman as rapidly as possible. The site was then covered with sterile drapes, after which the surgeon incised the skin in a line paralleling the patient's midline in such a fashion to include this bleeding site. Following this he rapidly dissected down through the various anatomic structures of this area of the neck and came upon the carotid artery. It was lacerated by the transiting bullet.

With some effort the surgeon was able to place a small hemostatic clamp of the vessel just proximal and distal to the bleeding site and secure the bleeding adequately. He then could close the lacerated artery with appropriate vascular suture material, whereupon he released the clamp and the blood again flowed through the artery into the left side of the brain and the left side of the head in an unrestricted fashion. After the wound was closed and the patient was removed to the intensive care unit, appropriate orders for the corpsman were written. The surgeon, whose name was Jim Rankin, and I then walked out along the sand to take a breather.

"You know, LT, you were working way outside your area

of expertise. You know that, don't you?" Jim said. He had a slight smile on his face, though I could see he was as exhausted as I was.

"Suppose so," I said. "Had to be done."

"Well, I'm going to report you to the Board of Medical Examiners wherever you end up when we get home," he said, smiling even more broadly. "That was a sorry performance in there."

"Then I'd best make sure to move to wherever you're not when we get back!" I said.

My peers and I often joked to ease the tension. We needed to.

On another occasion, a young marine had sustained a gunshot wound, which entered his abdomen and exited his back just to the left of the midline and barely missed his spinal cord. When he was brought in by the evacuation helicopter, he was still moving his legs with no difficulty. He, however, was rapidly going into shock, which to physicians simply means that his blood volume was decreased below a critical level, causing his blood pressure to drop very low and his pulse to become rapid. If this condition was not reversed quickly he would develop a cardiac arrest and die.

The patient was taken quickly to the operating room and placed under general anesthesia. While an operating room corpsman was cleansing his abdomen, the surgeons washed their hands rapidly, draped the patient with sterile towels, and opened the abdomen in the standard fashion to inspect the intestine. They found several penetration sites, closed them with suture material, and began the surgical closure. During this process, they looked behind his intestine and noticed that there was a puncture site from the bullet just to the left of his vertebra, proceeding outward toward his spinal canal.

At this point they were not certain that the lateral aspect

of his spinal cord had not been injured and requested that I come into the operating room and explore that site through their abdominal opening. I did so and satisfied myself that his spinal canal had not been violated and assured them that neurosurgical intervention would not be necessary.

Following completion of the procedure, the surgeon and I wandered over to the officers' club to review the experience and chide each other over who was the better surgeon. There were a few other situations where I did volunteer my services. Quite frankly, if I did not, the commanding officer of the hospital would have ordered me to cooperate.

Under those conditions I functioned as an intern and actually felt like one as I held retractors in various positions for varying lengths of time and reminisced about some six years earlier when, in fact, I was an intern. Many days during that year of training I held retractors for surgeons for different operations and for extended periods, never daring to utter a complaint that my arm was getting tired or inquiring of the surgeon as to the time at which he might finish the procedure so that I could go for a swim at the imaginary country club.

Functioning as an assistant, as any surgeon can attest, provides one with an opportunity to look about the operating room unencumbered and observe other events directly related to the OR scene. When one is the surgeon in charge, his attention is focused directly at the operating site, with most of his conversation aimed at the anesthesiologist in relation to the condition of the patient, or to the instrument nurse. Superficial remarks do arise as the pressure of the operation subsides. As an assistant, I had a better chance to observe the charged environment of this crude operating theater in a combat arena.

The hospital corpsmen assigned to the operating room were rushing back and forth, either acquiring more blood from the blood bank a hundred or so feet away or obtaining additional infusion tubing or drugs for the anesthesiologist attending the patient. Alternatively, they might be bringing in fresh and sterile sponges for the surgeons, as needed, at the operating table. This particular operation required the skill of a general and an orthopedic surgeon, and each needed an assistant plus a corpsman to hand instruments directly to the surgeon. We, therefore, had six people plus the anesthesiologist crowding around the battered, bleeding patient.

Sometimes I can see the scenes in the China Beach OR like they just happened yesterday. They are burned into my memory, all the more so when I wasn't the lead surgeon, as was the case in this operation. Amid the controlled chaos, I glanced up at the ceiling, which was about ten feet high, and squinted at the two bright lights mounted on a mobile track. The lighting was so much better than it had been at Charlie Med. The constant pinging of monitoring equipment associated with the anesthetic array, remarks by the surgeons regarding progress or a status request from the anesthesiologist, and the slam of the exit door as an equipment runner came or went—it all added to the low din.

Most of our cases involved a casualty with multiple injuries. Under these conditions the small operating room restricted to one end of a Quonset hut became rather crowded and notably busy. I also could observe the drapes around the patient, the operating room gowns on the surgeons in attendance, and the floor itself. The blood oozed from as many as four wounds and was soaking the patient's sterile drapes and the medical personnel's gowns. It was collecting at the bottom of the drapes and literally dripping like crimson rain to the concrete floor beneath the operating table. I followed it across the canted floor toward the drain site on one side of the OR. Simultaneous with the loss, an infusion of blood by the anesthesiologist was under way.

"Keep up with the blood loss," the lead surgeon demanded. "We're gonna lose him!"

I had many years of training in neurosurgery and additional experience in operating rooms as an intern and medical student in prior years, yet I never saw so much blood coming from patients who, by and large, not only survived the operations but progressed and returned to a reasonable state of health. This macabre-like scene was sometimes acted out several times a week, and the conversation at the operating table was usually sharp, to the point, and frequently abrasive by tense, straining surgeons.

Late one night I was awakened by a messenger from the shock tent that a major head injury had just been brought in by helicopter. I distinctly recall that there was a heavy rain with drops so big that they literally drummed on the metal surface of the Quonset, sounding much like the snare drum in an orchestra. I forced myself to surface from sleep, rubbed my eyes, quickly put on my uniform and boots, pulled on my poncho to shield the rain, and went out the door of the Quonset to an ultra-dark, steady monsoon. I got into the jeep (after dark we used jeeps with a driver to go across the sand dune to the patient care area), and I was driven directly up to the shock tent.

In the center of this emergency room Quonset was a single casualty, a marine, lying on one of the gurneys stretched across sawhorses and being ministered to by the anesthesiologist and three corpsmen.

Quickly I found a bullet wound of entrance just above his eyebrow on the right, with blood radiating in a spider leg-like fashion from it as he lay supine and unconscious on the stretcher. As the blood oozed out, so too did the so-characteristic gelatinous grayish-white brain material, telling me that there was a great deal of pressure building in his head, a deadly omen.

I got an X-ray in the lateral and anterior-posterior direction and was able to confirm that a single missile had entered just above his right eye and then traveled toward the back of his head, across the midline, and was lodged just on the inner side of his skull in what we call the occipital region. I assured myself that his pupils were still equal, indicating that he was potentially salvageable; however, I noted that he was demonstrating what we call "Decerebrate Rigidity" of one of his legs, which is a stiffening of the leg and extension of the foot and toe downward, an indication that there is irritation of part of the all-vital brain stem. I quickly surmised this was a result of the pressure of the swollen brain and blood collecting in his head, and I ordered everyone involved to take him directly to the operating room, where we would carry out cranial surgery.

While they were in the process of moving him, I quickly went to the designated surgery Quonset nearby to change from my uniform into a surgical gown and called for my frequent corpsmen assistant, Bart Bean. He arrived shortly, sleepy but ready. He also put on a surgical gown, whereupon we both went directly to the operating room. The anesthesiologist administrated anesthesia and intubated the victim. He stated that the young man's condition was "unstable."

I positioned him in a supine orientation so that I was looking directly down at the wound of entrance above his right eye. I shaved his hair from his ears forward and advised one of the corpsmen to cleanse the scalp around the wound while Bart and I scrubbed our hands. We did so rapidly in view of the urgency of the situation, put on our sterile gowns and gloves, and then placed the sterile drapes around the wound so as to create a sterile instrument arrangement adjacent to the operating table. I then instructed the circulating corpsman to bring the electrocautery unit adjacent to the operating table so that I could cauterize bleeding sites as I encountered them. I arranged the overhead operating light as best I could and asked for the scalpel. Based on the trajectory of the wound, I decided that I would make a long S-shaped incision from the wound of entrance backward across the top of his head just in front of the ears.

I incised the scalp, and bleeding points developed; however, they were easily stopped with electrocautery. I then rapidly separated the edges of the scalp widely so as to expose the underlying skull and the bullet hole. Several fracture lines around the wound site came into view and radiated much like earthquake faults in an erratic fashion.

Using an instrument that looks something like pliers with sharp-biting edges on it we call a "rongeur," I systematically bit away (so to speak) pieces of bone, starting at the bullet penetration site and proceeding backward and laterally so as to expose the membranes surrounding the brain cells called the Dura Mater. In this fashion I unroofed the skull adjacent to the bullet hole in front to a point halfway back along his head, in a trench-like fashion. Thus, I felt that I had most of the region that might cause considerable bleeding exposed, and I was ready to deal with blood loss of a sharp nature if it should occur. I then retracted the edge of this parchment-like Dura with sutures both to the right and to the left of this long trench-like opening. The brain was now exposed and was observed to be both hemorrhagic-looking and swollen. In fact, much of it was beginning to ooze from the opening I had just made. Again, rapidly with the electrocautery, I cut into the swollen brain, beginning where the bullet entered, and directed the incision in a trench-like fashion.

At this point, using the suction equipment, a slender vacuum rubber tubing connected to a spear-shaped sterile tip that Bart had made for me, I was able to aspirate swollen, lifeless brain material that had the appearance of beaten egg white and the viscosity of gelatin. I continued to work and evacuate damaged—or what we call devitalized—brain aligned along the bullet track.

As I proceeded, bleeding from the bullet track itself increased in severity. Ordinarily, with the aid of aspiration equipment, I could rapidly proceed down into this bleeding site, identify the bleeding vessel, and control with the electrocautery. The maneuver was unsuccessful this time, however, and the bleeding continued.

I advised the anesthesiologist that bleeding was more than I had expected and ordered him to begin to infuse blood. He did so, and the patient's blood pressure came up some. I felt better. The bleeding persisted, however, and I was forced to more aggressively pursue the bleeding point down in the center of the bullet track. In doing so, I found only more and more profuse bleeding points and more and more swelling. I then more vigorously and rapidly used the electrocautery, stopping bleeding points as rapidly as they seemed to arise. The bleeding slowed down, and I took a measure of comfort since I felt more certain that I had the situation under control.

His brain was still badly swollen, however, and it is an uncontested principle of neurosurgery that it must be relaxed and pulsating, so to speak (a function of the pulsatile action of the heart), before one closes a wound. Should this principle not be adhered to, the patient will not survive the severe pressure building in the head. It literally crushes the brain.

I now proceeded to remove more brain from the right side of the missile track, which I knew from my training in neurophysiology was a relatively benign area in the sense that an individual could lose some parts of his brain and yet function relatively well. This portion of the operation proceeded well. However, suddenly from the original bullet track toward the back of the head and the deep cavity of my operative site, more intense bleeding erupted. I quickly returned to this site and used my suction equipment to aspirate away the blood. I used the electrocautery equipment to control the hemorrhagic sites. I desperately attempted to identify the source of bleeding and bring this critical state again under control. The operation had now taken on a demonic aura. Despite my best efforts, bleeding continued. To aggravate the situation, blood began to flow from the envelope between the parchment-like Dura over the brain and beneath the skull. This was beyond the limits of the skull opening I had made. I was now dealing with bleeding from two hidden sites, and it intensified.

I labored desperately to control the situation, now of crisis dimensions, but the anesthesiologist advised me that the blood pressure was again beginning to drop.

Fully aware that removing more brain would increase the patient's neurologic disability subsequent to surgery, it was my decision that I had no choice but to do just that. I did so and was able to control some of the bleeding from deep in the wound site; however, the bleeding from the hidden site between the skull and the Dural covering well beyond the limits of my skull opening persisted unabated.

I employed every surgical maneuver I was trained to bring to bear on such a situation; however, blood loss continued, and despite blood infusion by the anesthesiologist, blood pressure began to plummet to critical levels. I used sponges to control the bleeding to the extent possible; however, each surgical effort was fraught with frustration, and his blood pressure continued to fail. I instructed the anesthesiologist to run the blood infusion as fast as possible and then began to rongeur away more of the skull opening in the direction of the bleeding in a effort to identify the massive bleeding source and bring it under control.

I now recognized what had happened. The scattered earthquake-like fault lines I described earlier in the operation had no doubt torn open one of the major blood-draining sinuses from the brain, conducting blood to the jugular veins in the neck and into the great veins of the chest and ultimately the heart. Unfortunately, however, the point where one of these large draining sinuses had been lacerated was well beyond my operative view, and I could not gain control.

The only option was to pack small sponges between the skull and the parchment-like Dura to dam off (so to speak) the bleeding. However, his blood pressure continued to deteriorate. Suddenly the anesthesiologist advised me that we had a cardiac arrest.

Quickly the corpsmen pulled the drapes off the chest while I tried to control bleeding in the head. The anesthesiologist and one of the corpsmen began to apply alternating mechanical compression over the lower part of his chest. They continued this for several minutes while I, openly frustrated, worked feverishly to control the bleeding in the head.

The situation remained out of control, and after fifteen minutes of pumping the chest, and recognition that I was dooming this man to a coffin, I instructed everyone to cease. At this moment, silence enveloped the operating room. The drum-like beating of the rain on the metal roof continued and remained the only sounds. The patient lay supine, blood still dripping from his head down the blue-green operating drapes and by now had formed a large red collection of crimson-colored fluid on the concrete floor.

All of us stood in dismay, staring at this young man, drained of blood and of his life. This was not the first time this had happened to me in Vietnam, nor was it the last. After a time I regained some composure and advised the corpsman to call for a body bag and move the corpse across the compound to the Quonset, where the dead bodies were maintained.

I knew that in a few days a stunned mother would receive a stuffed coffin in exchange for the child she once nurtured. If the man had a girlfriend, she'd learn that the man she loved was dead, and she would be forever scarred in some way. It was about four thirty in the morning as I slowly turned toward the door of the operating Quonset, peeled off my blood-soaked operating room gown and gloves, and then looked down and saw my black boots and socks literally soaked in the deep red color of fresh blood.

I walked out of the operating room and across the wooden walkway under the flat corrugated metal rain protector that spanned between the various patient-care and administrative Quonsets. The rain continued to beat down on the corrugated awning. In the catty-corner Quonset, which was the surgeon's dressing area, I stripped off my gown and noted that some of the blood had actually soaked through from the sterile scrub gown to my operating scrub suit. I completed my operative note on the patient's chart, describing the event. I knew from the beginning this injury was very dangerous. Even with the significant surgical experience I had accumulated in recent months, I was still over my head, and it really hurt.

I then put on my uniform, rubbed the blood off my boots as much as possible with the scrub gown I had just taken off, and threw it in a pile for the laundry. Then I walked back out of the Quonset, again under the protective metal corrugated awning, to the security building, where I was given a ride in a covered jeep back to my Quonset in the pounding rain.

I got out, thanked the driver, and quickly retreated into

the dark Quonset. I stumbled over to my bunk, lay down flat on my back, clothes still on, and stared directly up into the pitch darkness, listening to the pounding rain on the roof that was almost synchronous with the haunted and anguished voice echoing over and over in my mind: "Failed! Failed! Failed!"

In reality, the complexity of this particular patient's injury was likely beyond the capability of any neurosurgeon I have known. Somehow, though, I took no comfort in this knowledge. The fact that it happened to me meant I would live with his death as a haunting experience and a bitter memory for the rest of my life. I knew that then, and it turns out I was correct. There are some scenes from China Beach I will never forget, and the death of that kid is one of them. After several such heartbreaking experiences, I began to weave a mental image of a cast of characters lined up in coffins and moving toward an inferno. The corpses looked over their shoulder, blaming me.

At times like that, I don't know how I kept myself together, but somehow I managed. I'd recall the comment of Sir Clifford Allbutt, an English professor of surgery who contributed much to the early field of modern medicine: "Let me remind you how fertile the blood of warriors is in rearing good surgeons." But at what price was I learning my profession? At what cost to the kids who came to me torn apart with massive injuries from the battlefield? Even survivors paid dearly on some occasions.

A neurosurgeon is taught to respect the certain critical areas of the brain during operations. Regrettably, the fragments hurled by exploding hand grenades, land mines, artillery shells, and bullets have no respect for such critical areas. Time and time again I found myself delving into these areas to control bleeding lest the trooper die. The results, if both the patient and I were fortunate, would be a salvaged life. Too often, however, the patient would lose part of his cognitive abilities. Too often the pieces of metal from exploded weapons were driven deep into a critical region of his brain, and I could do nothing but let him die. Unquestionably, the longer I was at China Beach, the more it seemed practical and imperative to sometimes make decisions that some would say only God could make. I certainly did not go around trying to play God, but sometimes I simply could not salvage the poor kid on the table.

I always tried to save the life of the marine; I did everything I could to ensure that he would be a functioning person after he recovered from surgery. All too often these two objectives were in conflict. Yet I had to do this while in the center of a charged situation with a marine in a coma from a bullet in his head. His brain was swelling by the moment, and brain tissue was oozing from the bullet site like toothpaste, and I had to decide. *Do I operate now or let him die?*

Usually I would go for it. If I was right and a vital center was not involved, I could bring a man from death. If I was wrong and found a hopeless condition when I got inside his brain, I created a permanent cripple. Failing to meet the principles of surgical management of penetrating head injuries would doom the patient to either death or, worse, a nursing home. Many times I evaluated a patient and ascertained within a short time that one or more missiles were lodged in various parts of the brain. Then I either operated or I did not.

This quandary haunted me my entire time in Vietnam. Of the many adversities that I faced in Vietnam, all paled in comparison to the agonizing realization that resonated through my psyche as I prepared a patient for surgery.

He may end up a cripple or a vegetable. He may hate me for saving him!

After a difficult operation, when I would wonder if the soldier would wake up at all or if he'd wake up so brain damaged that his life was essentially over, I'd walk off to my quarters, feeling about as terrible as I think I've ever felt then or since. I would ignore the ride in the security jeep and head out over the sand dunes in the dark hours of the early morning, bathed in the continued flares dropped from aircraft to scare off the Viet Cong. I barely noticed the *thud* of distant artillery or the not-so-distant crack of rifle fire and kicked the sand in frustration.

As I slowly walked, I thought many somber things. *If I never joined the navy and never set foot in this damned country, would not many of my patients be better off stilled in their graves? Would not that be better than languishing in a nursing home in Chicago, Dallas, Cleveland, or wherever? Doomed to their exile with little or no brain function, a living corpse.*

I longed to see the stars on nights like that. Instead I could only see the dull yellowish light of flares, while the grand expanse of heavens was lost to me.

15

COMBAT

IT WAS LATE DUSK, AND JUST a thin pink band of light offered illumination of the hills to the west while the last stabbing streaks of sunlight were disappearing. I'd completed a surgical procedure about half an hour ago. I planned to return to quarters to lie in the rack or write a letter home and describe beautiful Hawaii in the evening to keep up the deception I'd decided upon to keep my elderly parents from worrying about me. They still thought I was in Hawaii, and that was good. Dusk was about to surrender to the night, and the warm dry air was motionless. The diesel generators, strategically positioned here and there on the compound, continued to growl their low-frequency rumble.

Comfortable with the result of my surgical case, I nonchalantly walked from the operating room across the wooden walkway into the intensive care unit, where I wrote my brief operative note, followed by postoperative orders, and then saw to it that he was stable in his rack. Then I walked out of ICU onto the hard-packed gravel and sand surface in the direction of my quarters.

There were no incoming casualties and no helicopters standing on the landing pad. Indeed, for this place it seemed like serenity.

I met two corpsmen in the vicinity and stopped for a moment to chat. In the distance, as usual, we could hear artillery batteries rumble. Overhead at about 3,000 feet one could see the very familiar remnants of three to four parachute flares drifting slowly to earth. The hospital had been running for months and had not been directly threatened; thus, not many of us bothered to wear our sidearms when we left our quarters to go one hundred or so yards to the patient-care area.

We had become complacent. While the war was all around us, we ignored it. Then it happened. First from my right at one hundred yards, then behind me about fifty yards, and now on the left and in front at fifty yards or so came the unmistakable ear-shattering explosions of incoming mortar rounds. Instinctively, the three of us dropped down against the packed sand. Surely, if I could have used my nose as a cutting blade, it would have burrowed into the hard gravel-like earth for several feet. One can't get close enough to the earth at such a time. But I couldn't get deeper! The diesel generators fell silent. An ominous silence! Then the lights went out and, except for the distant aerial flares, we were in inky darkness. The raid siren wailed in the distance. Again, the pounding thump of more incoming fire drove us closer to the earth. This was for real, and we were in deep trouble!

At this point in my tour of Vietnam I had stood witness to slashed and mangled bodies of at least two hundred marines who were near exploding mortar rounds. Many died! Now I was in the same boat, and the very idea struck terror in my heart. *The next incoming round may be the one that kills me and slices the remains into several steaks.* Lying there facedown, I knew I could not burrow any deeper into the hard ground. Imprisoned by mortar rounds bursting around us—some close, others at a distance—all shaking the very earth beneath us, I was terror stricken.

I surely had seen death in others hundreds of times, and now was it to be my turn? One pities those in abject danger, but when it is your turn, the feeling is terror. I knew intuitively that if the next round hit within ten feet of us, I would die instantly and would never feel it. I also knew from vicarious experience that if it hit twenty to forty feet away, it would send supersonic metal particles in all directions, including mine, knifing through skin, muscle, bone, intestines, and leaving me a bleeding hulk possibly to survive as a cripple or, worse still, linger awhile and then die. These thoughts only enhanced the terror. As I buried my face for protection as close as possible against the hard-packed sandy surface and scratched at the ground with my fingers to carve some sort of a cover, I noticed blood welling up under my fingernails.

From the earliest days of medical school, we embryonic physicians progressively grew aware of the complex interactions of the human machine, including the interdependence of one system upon another. Following this we studied the concept of pathophysiology, which is the mechanism of dysfunction of the body and all the nasty aspects of injury to a person. The pain, the fear, the nausea, the total loss of human dignity as one offers himself up on the altar of medical science are real. Such things as myriads of needles, merciless pokes here and there, the multiplicity of tests including gases and fluids shoved in either end of our alimentary track, and the fearsome-looking testing machines that stare menacingly at us as we are rolled into various examining rooms were all visible. All were magnified at this moment.

Following this, a stern gray-haired doctor in a long white coat with a stethoscope around his neck walks in and tells us that we had an injury or a disease process that is relentless if not stopped at hell's door by a painful or sickening drug protocol or a complicated operation that itself might snuff out our life or leave us maimed forever. He then says sternly, "Sign here so that we can get on with it."

Now, rather than my usual role as the doctor of distressing news, I may be confronted with the reality of being that patient. At this instant, I truly envied the marines who were unaware of the true fragility of the human being. They are, under these circumstances, more cavalier, secure in an opaque view that, should they be struck down by the enemy, the navy doctors are just a short helicopter trip away and can restore them to their original state of well-being.

Now I, Paul Pitlyk, was in harm's way and quite possibly would cycle through the shock tent on a stretcher, IV fluids running, bleeding from various parts of my torn body, and destined for an operating room with uncertain results.

I prayed and asked God to take my body to heaven after it is blown to hell. To be sure he heard me, I prayed this time out loud. The two corpsmen beside me made little sound. I certainly didn't care if they did hear my pleadings!

We all know we are going to die, and the fortunate of us experience it unexpectedly and suddenly, or basking in senility, or are humanely sedated in a hospital to await the death call. To be fully cognizant of your situation the instant before death, in my opinion, is fraught with the twin cataclysm of fear and hopelessness.

It had been drilled repeatedly into our minds that the policy of the enemy in offensive actions was to wait until just after dark, launch a mortar barrage, and then with infantry-carrying satchel charges, run across the compound, cut down defending forces, and hopefully disable the compound with these explosive charges. They then kill as many personnel as possible and quickly shrink back into the inky darkness.

When the mortars ceased, the hospital personnel immediately went into their defined posture while the marine platoon were rapidly assuming predefined positions to protect the hospital. The hospital personnel, as advised, forcibly took all patients off their racks and pushed them regardless of their condition (connecting IVs or respiratory lines) under their racks on the plywood floor in an effort to afford some element of protection.

We were then charged with the responsibility to protect as well as possible the wounded troops. The corpsmen quickly accomplished this. We now became acutely conscious of a deafening silence, from the now-mute diesel generators and the cessation of incoming mortar rounds. Indeed, it was our expectation that within moments we would be dealing face-to-face with enemy troops.

I knew that there was no way that I could make my way in the dark one hundred or so yards to my bunk area to procure my weapon. With the two corpsmen, therefore, I crawled with nose in the dirt to the nearest Quonset hut. A rat could not have gotten closer to the ground then I did that night!

We then worked our way to the door at the end. Again while in the prone position, I reached upward and pulled on the handle of the door to open it. We immediately were met with the business end of a rifle held by a marine who also was lying in the prone position waiting for the enemy. I did not appreciate this, but this was no time to argue. I quickly identified the three of us, and he allowed us in. After we crawled in, a battle lamp was turned on by someone, whereupon I found myself staring directly at, and being glared back at by, at least fifteen different men. One of them identified himself as a navy chief petty officer and indicated that the rest of them were either hospital corpsmen or marines who had weapons. They just happened to be on the compound for one reason or another when we were hit.

I distinctly remember saying to the chief, "Why are they all looking at me?"

His response was terse. "You are in charge, sir."

I knew that physicians are some of the least equipped people for command. And I was scared to death. I said, "Chief, what should I do?"

Again, his response was brief and emotionless. "Don't look so scared, sir."

I got just a bit sharp with him and his laconic attitude. Then I said, "If you will turn off the goddamn light, I won't look so scared."

He turned off the lantern and said, "We are awaiting your instructions, sir!"

By that time in my career I had enough experience to know that a senior officer always has an obligation to demonstrate confidence and forcefulness in front of the men. In the next thirty seconds, my mind worked feverishly. Fully conversant of the fact that I had not been trained by the navy to lead troops, I therefore chose to reenact a vicarious experience from the "movie theater" and said to myself, "What would John Wayne do?" To my amazement, a tactical plan bounded into my psyche, whereupon I stood up with artificial confidence.

"Turn that battle lamp back on!" I said, my voice as insistent as I could make it. "Put a sentry at either door of the Quonset, and instruct them to level anyone who attempts to enter forcibly without my okay."

I then instructed him to place a sentry adjacent to each of the four side windows, which were standard on Quonsets, and ordered them to shoot anyone who tried to crawl through. Once the sentries were in place, I said, "Now turn that lamp off, Chief!"

He complied.

The place fell into deep silent darkness while I slithered into a corner on the floor. While I certainly wasn't getting my ego stroked, I didn't like the beating it was taking either. To my relief, about thirty minutes later a voice speaking perfect English said in an authoritative yet relatively low voice through one of the closed doors, "I am a marine lieutenant and demand to come aboard."

That was enough for me. I ordered him to be let in and immediately relinquished all responsibility to this young stern-looking officer in battle dress and holding a .45-caliber handgun menacingly in his right hand. A sense of relief came across my face much like a cool breeze. I suspect that the other men in the Quonset also felt relieved but for another reason—now they did not have to trust their survival to a terror-stricken, inept doctor, a travesty of a commander.

By now it had been one hour since the mortar barrage had stopped, and we had not detected enemy troops coming across the concertina wire or, possible worse, already in our midst and now working their way between the Quonsets with their weapons and satchel charges. I moved out of the Quonset after my brief tenure as a "marine commanding officer," and, even though it was pitch dark, was able to make contact with the chief of surgery and the hospital commander who advised me as to the status of the enemy.

We rather foolishly remained standing upright, adjacent to another Quonset, when a loud explosion from another impacting missile struck about thirty yards from us, causing a flash that transiently blinded me. Of course, in a Pavlovian fashion, the three of us fell facedown onto the sand and gravel surface. It was the closest explosion of the entire event, and I am amazed that not one of the three of us sustained penetrating fragment injuries. No additional rounds were incoming, and within about five minutes we were advised that this was a friendly outgoing round that had been launched from behind our camp. It was tersely referred to as a "short round" by our marines and unceremoniously dismissed.

The enemy chose not to overrun the compound that night for reasons that remain an enigma to me today; however, it was brought to our attention by the intelligence section the next day that their intent was not to attack and destroy a hospital, but rather to launch the mortar rounds on the marine helicopter facility directly adjacent to our compound and destroy as many aircraft as possible.

The patients were put back on their racks, grumbling and complaining. I heard one patient grumble that he had not come here to be treated this way. IVs were restarted, frayed nerves of the attending staff were steadied, and many of us echoed a hollow laugh that more appropriately sounded much like gallows humor. All among us had seen the results of exploding mortars on so many patients and were fully versed with the crippling, maiming, and death-dealing characteristics of this fearsome weapon.

Although few slept well that night, by the next day we were functioning in our usual, reasonably professional fashion. The war came a bit closer that night. Everyone wore their cartridge belt with a holstered .45-caliber handgun, whether we were making rounds on patients, going back to our quarters, or even going to the latrine. I distinctly recall cleaning my weapon four times the next day after having ignored that greasy piece of steel for many weeks. The next morning I was struck with the thought that I was a member of the Department of Defense of the most powerful nation on earth yet was forced by virtue of military incompetence and tactical ignorance to mimic the behavior of an action-oriented movie star in an effort to orderly manage an actual combat event.

The fear of getting killed diminished greatly after I left Charlie Med, and except for the mortar attack at China Beach I generally did not walk around fearing the worst. You could even say I got bored on occasions. For instance, one day I let boredom get the best of me and almost paid dearly for it.

At this point in my tour in Vietnam, I had flown on the medevac helicopters for the purposes of consulting at the marine hospital about twenty miles from us and was relatively familiar with the craft. I must admit that whenever I saw a helicopter coming in, I was somewhat envious of the pilots and the crew who no doubt led a life of adventure and excitement.

One afternoon, things were quiet, and a curiosity and desire to fly captured my interest. I just wanted to fly out and about in a Huey. A trip over the countryside would be just great, or so I thought. After all, the helo base was a short walk out of the hospital gate, right? I simply wandered out the front gate of our hospital to the helicopter base immediately next to us, went into the operations tent, identified myself, and inquired as to whether I might take a ride on one of the Hueys the next time it was going out.

I was told that a group of two gunships routinely patrolled various sectors within an area of fifty miles, providing on-site fire support for ground marines should it be needed. The operations officer advised me that he had no objection to me flying along if I so desired. I was delighted!

After being briefed in the chopper on its air characteristics and how to react in case of an emergency, I was set. I was taken over to the equipment tent about twenty-five yards from where the craft stood and provided with a flight suit, which is a long set of coveralls made of a fireproof material, a flight helmet through which I could listen or speak to the pilots via incorporated earphones and a microphone, and a pair of fireproof gloves. I was already wearing the required boots. Next, I was escorted out of the tent to the flight line, where the two gunships next in line for a patrol mission were being readied for flight. I was shown where to sit in the craft and advised what to expect.

As I've said, these choppers afforded the pilots and observer fabulous views of the countryside. You could also look out the broad side doors, which were kept open during flight. My position was a relatively small seat into which I was strapped behind the two pilots. The pilots got in and strapped themselves in, as did the two gunners on either side and behind me. I watched the pilots, through a sequence of maneuvers, turn on the gas turbine engine, and the large rotor blade above us began to spin.

About one hundred yards in front of us was our sister craft doing the same thing. We all wore flight helmets, including the earphones via which I could hear all conversations between the pilots and incoming radio communications from the other ship or from ground personnel with radios. In addition, I had a small mouthpiece. I didn't say a damn word.

The signal to go was radioed from the small control tower, and both aircraft lifted about two feet off the ground and moved forward slowly toward the end of the runway, where each then settled again on the landing matting. The gunners on either side stepped out of the craft and reached down on the rocket pods and then made some adjustment. I found out later this was the process of arming these weapons.

After this they got back in and strapped themselves in, and both craft lifted rather effortlessly from the ground, moved ever so slowly forward and then more rapidly while gaining altitude. I watched the runway sink away from below us as the helicopters banked to the right, such that I could look downward with no difficultly. It was a sunny day, with the South China Sea off to our left, shimmering like diamonds. Forward and to our right was first the wide and sandy beach area that gradually gave way to increased foliage and finally thick jungle through which one could only occasionally see the ground. The copters continued to fly inland with the ground level rising as the countryside gradually turned to low mountainous terrain.

I could hear banter between the two pilots similar to that one hears on a Sunday afternoon drive. There was the smell of jet fumes, and it was not offensive. I felt the wind dashing against my face. I looked behind, and the two gunners looked bored. Off to our right and ahead about two hundred yards was our sister ship just swimming along. I was really enjoying this "jaunt" in the sky.

As we flew, a pilot spoke to me and advised that this was referred to as a "perimeter run," whereby we would fly around a certain sector for a specified period of time, following which, if we were not needed by ground troops for fire support, we would simply return to base. He indicated that the trip was generally quite boring; however, the countryside was worth seeing and drinking in. I enjoyed the beautiful green countryside sliding below us at our assigned altitude of about 1,500 feet.

The two helicopters reached their appointed patrol location and began to make wide orbits while monitoring radio traffic from the marine ground forces in that particular sector. I estimated the orbit to be a rough circle about twenty to twenty-five miles. For a while we simply cruised uneventfully, watching the terrain move beneath us, which was now an admixture of both thick forest and jungle plus a narrow meandering river and scattered rice paddies on a distant mesa.

The sun shone brightly, the sky was blue, the ground below was jade green, and the narrow river snaking its way through the countryside was greenish brown. Occasionally as we flew, I heard crackling static through earphones in my flight helmet. I understood only the voice of one of the pilots talking to the other about some mundane subject. It seems almost as if they were trying to pass the time. Indeed, I too was becoming complacent; however, as I looked off into the distance directly ahead of the chopper, I could see a plume of bluish smoke rising from some sort of a building-like structure on the bank of the river. A moment later, a crackling male voice came over the radio, calling for "Roseanne."

The pilot instantly responded, indicating that Roseanne was available, which I assume was the radio signature of our helicopter. More chatter took place, and things began to happen. Immediately the pilot banked the craft rather sharply to the right and began to descend toward the edge of one of the rice paddies, where I could see a series of small huts or hamlets.

The pilot continued to dive, aiming the craft directly at one hamlet while folding down in front of him a device mounted much like the sun visor of an automobile. It was, in fact, a gun sight. Indeed, with this sighting device he could aim the craft directly at a target of interest.

I was impressed to see the pilot very calmly reach into the left upper pocket of his flight suit, pull out a pack of cigarettes, extract one from the package, and light it with a lighter while angling the plane toward the target. He then tipped the nose downward to point, as if it was a rifle, directly at a target.

An instant later he pressed the trigger on his control

stick, and the twin machine guns on either side of the craft erupted into a continuous explosive chatter. Even with the sound-muting devices in our flight helmets, the noise was deafening. Again a crackling voice came over the radio, cautioning Roseanne that heavy fire was being directed at our aircraft from the series of hamlets and to take great caution. Neither pilot flinched.

I could see tracers of fire from our craft directed at the target since every several rounds coming from a machine gun was a tracer round and, thus, appeared as a small red dot heading for the enemy in the hamlets.

At about two hundred feet over the ground, the pilot pulled back abruptly on the control stick, banked the craft hard to the left to pull it up and away from the target, following which our companion helicopter followed a similar course and fired upon the target in a similar fashion. Our craft continued to bank to the left while climbing in the distance, getting ready to orbit back for another run.

I had spent a limited amount of time in aircraft, either helicopters or airplanes, in Vietnam. Up until this date, however, I had never been engaged in direct air-to-ground combat. As the craft angled down toward the target a second time, and its guns again began barking, I noted the bright-red sparkle of rapidly moving particles directly toward us from the target itself. Enemy gunfire! This was not a routine joyride. *What the hell am I doing up here!*

An adrenaline rush ensued, blood pumped through my head, and every part of my body felt as if it were electricity. The closer we dove at the target, the more apparent was the flickering fire from the enemy below. Would the pilot never pull up the nose? Would he fly directly into the target? Now more apparent was the flickering fire from the enemy below. *Is he crazy? I'm gonna die!* Time seemed interminable! Just as quickly as he began to dive, he pulled the cyclic back toward his abdomen, and the craft promptly angled upward and away from the menacing enemy. I breathed a sigh of relief that I had survived a close encounter with my Maker. However, the pilot banked sharply to the left, climbed a bit, banked again to the left, and dove directly at the target. My heart sank to my stomach. I sat in frozen terror, again watching and hearing our guns thunder at the opposition and theirs angrily barking back. *This pilot is crazy! I am too!* Which one of those flickering red tracer bullets would come crashing through this complex yet fragile aircraft, causing confusion, then twisting, turning, and rolling as it plummeted to the earth?

Again, after the shrieking dive and thundering machine guns, the pilot pulled the cyclic back into his abdomen and the ship again angled up and away from the target. The first few times that he made a pass I thought I was going to die; however, when he made a fourth and even closer run at the target, I was certain that I had seen my last sunrise, had done my last operation, and never would set foot in my home again. I had studied and trained for so many years and then come halfway around the world to be graciously accepted into the glorious heavens that had been described so elegantly by the nuns in grade school.

Alternatively, though, I might find myself trapped for all eternity in the jaws of hell. It was too late to make amends for all the wrong I had done, and there had been quite a litany of such transgressions. All I could do now was plead forgiveness in the few moments yet available to do so. I was a victim of thirst for excitement and now a prisoner of the same. What was left would be stuffed into a coffin. All these thoughts resonated in repetition through my disintegrating psyche.

We again fired at the target for approximately twenty to twenty-five seconds before the wretched machine lurched upward, angled to the left, and prepared for yet another run. I believe we made eight or so runs at the target before it was decided that all enemy activity had been silenced. Our craft and wingman then climbed back up to about 1,500 feet and began to head back toward our helicopter base. En route, the pilot turned, looked back to me, and said in a very cool, flippant manner, "Doc, you don't know how lucky you are. Sometimes we go out here for a week before we get into a scrap like that."

At this point, my terror had been reduced to intense fright and finally disbelief that I had put myself in such a predicament. However, when I watched the pilot again reach into a pocket of his flight suit, pull out a pack of cigarettes, and light one up with a cigarette lighter, my fright came under control and my mind was again reverted to a semblance of reality. I was shaking vigorously. I thought about what the hell tempted me to wander over to the helicopter base, looking for such excitement.

It took about twenty to twenty-five minutes to fly back to our base, where both helicopters landed uneventfully. The engines were shut down, and I found the sudden silence deafening. I lifted off my helmet, loosened my seat belt, and crept out of the side of the craft. I stood up hesitantly and admittedly staggered about twenty-five yards over to the equipment tent, where each of us deposited our gear.

I was about to leave the equipment tent and walk back across the sand to the hospital latrine, when a marine master sergeant approached. He was already aware of the combat the two helicopters had encountered and was also aware that a local navy doctor was joyriding. He came up to me in a belligerent way, stating that I could easily have lost my life out there, which would be unfortunate; however, many future wounded marines would have been deprived of neurological care in the hiatus between my death and the time it took the navy to move another neurosurgeon from the United States.

Although somewhat irritated at his hostile attitude, I had to agree with him that no benefit to the military services was accrued by my helicopter ride on that afternoon. I accepted his admonition and walked back to the hospital, still feeling shaken and slightly nauseated. I walked up to a "piss tube" and unleashed a torrent. Two points circled through my brain: One, getting into that flying coffin was one of the dumbest things I'd ever done, and two, I could have died that day.

Pair of Huey gunships preparing for mission

Huey gunship approaching target

Pilot view Huey gunship near target

16

SUMMER HEAT

THE SUMMER OF 1966 WAS AN eventful one during my tour of duty in Vietnam. Yet, in many ways, those months blended in with the others into a strange sort of blur. That's how they strike me now, and I believe I felt a similar pattern back then. What most impressed me during my entire tour of duty was the bravery of the marines I met. These men were nothing short of heroic. Even when they had been badly wounded, most said they wanted to get back in the fight if they could.

I remember helping attend to a young man, a first lieutenant who had been shot through the chest. We confirmed with a chest X-ray that he had a pneumothorax on the left, which means that he had a collection of air between his chest wall and his lung, caused by a bullet into the chest, such that the lung was being compressed and could not expand for breathing purposes. Fortunately, humans have two lungs, and he was thus able to semi-function with the other one. It was necessary, though, to reinflate the damaged side to avoid complications.

In most cases, this can be accomplished by simply inserting a suction tube through the chest wall exterior of the lung and then connecting a suction apparatus to a vacuum pump, thereby allowing the lung to expand against the inner chest wall by virtue of the vacuum. This allows the patient to breathe normally. After healing efforts provided by Mother Nature, the leak in the lung itself seals, and the chest tubes can be removed. Following such, patients generally do well.

While this patient was being prepared for insertion of the chest tube, he was able to tell us something about where he had been and what had happened. They had been in a firefight with the enemy, in which he and many of his men were hit. This marine on the stretcher looked really banged up but was alert as a corpsman pulled off his boots, socks, and underwear.

"Haven't had my clothes off in two weeks," he said, and he seemed happy the clothing was gone.

While it struck me that he was glad to be rid of his dirty, blood-soaked uniform, it also struck me that he was embarrassed about how he looked. It was highly inappropriate for a marine, be he enlisted or officer, to appear less than impeccable.

On another occasion, a young marine was brought in after sustaining a leg injury. I was there to help other medical personnel in the shock Quonset. In the course of his medical evaluation and decisions regarding his management, I attempted to engage in a short conversation with him.

"I'm just a private, sir," he said.

The trooper indicated that I should first tend to the marines who outranked him. I was shocked and a little irritated that he would think I'd consider him less important than his superiors. I almost said something but thought better of it. To this day, he has my deep admiration, wherever he may be.

On another occasion, I was called from my sleeping quarters to see a marine gunnery sergeant, a member of a tank battalion. I walked into the shock tent, and there was sitting a large, strongly built forty-five-year-old. He was about six two, deeply tanned, and looking depressed.

He had not been injured but rather simply reported to the hospital after getting a ride in from his tank battalion headquarters several miles out in the jungle. I listened to his complaints, which included difficulty walking more than one hundred yards without developing rather intense aching low back and bilateral leg pain. I carried out a complete neurological exam, obtained an X-ray of his lumbar back, and was able to conclude that he had a condition we call lumbar stenosis. This is a disabling condition that usually requires surgery.

"You have something called lumbar stenosis, Sergeant. It's your ticket home," I said.

"Doc, just give me some pills. I'm going back to the unit."

"You won't be able to run as fast if you have to get away from your burning tank in a firefight," I said. "You're putting yourself and your men at risk."

"Just give me the pills, sir!"

I gave it a little thought and then made my decision. We needed men like that out in the bush, men who were committed, notwithstanding their own pain. I shook my head in a combination of dismay and admiration. I ordered the corpsman to provide him with appropriate analgesic medication, whereupon he stood up, saluted me, turned on his heels, and stalked out to the landing pad, where a marine jeep was waiting to take him back to his unit.

On still another occasion, I was just going about my

business when a naval administrative officer from the commanding officer's Quonset rushed up to me, asking to report directly to the shock tent for a neurological evaluation on a VIP. I walked quickly to the area, and as I approached it I saw a UH-1 helicopter standing on the helipad with the engine shut down. *This is unusual.* Both pilots were sitting in the cockpit.

I looked quizzically at them and then turned and walked into the shock tent, where the patient who was waiting just happened to be the commanding general of all the marines in Vietnam. Obviously, I was shocked to see him, and I must admit it was the first time I had ever seen him at close range. He was about fifty-five years old, wore a crew cut like all marines, displayed a rather ruddy coarse face, was at least six two, and must have weighed 225 pounds. Less than 15 percent of that weight was fat. His expression telegraphed no emotion, yet when he spoke it was in a commanding way.

He sat on the side of a stretcher, wearing a typical marine utility or jungle uniform and told me he had a pain radiating down his arm. I asked him to take off his uniform from the waist up, which he did promptly. He stood, and I quickly noticed at least four or five scars across his chest and shoulders, the shortest of which was four to five inches. They were quite old. I wondered about their origin; however, they were not causing the pain down his arm, and I was not about to ask a two-star general about the genesis of ancient trauma. I then examined him relative to the arm pain, obtained a cervical spine X-ray that demonstrated cervical spurs, and advised the general that the pain was emanating from a spur or disc in his neck, which was pinching the nerve going into his arm and causing him pain.

His response was "Doctor, I'm awful busy. Please give

me some pills so I can carry on my job, and I'll get out of your way."

I instructed the corpsman to obtain from the pharmacy the prescription that I wrote out, which included analgesics appropriate to control his pain, yet would not impair decision making or judgment. He put his uniform back on, said, "Thank you, Doctor," and walked out to his helicopter. Off he went!

I turned to one of the administrative officers who had attended the evaluation and asked about the source of the scars on his shoulders and chest. He told me that the general had served on Guadalcanal during the Second World War, where he had been wounded, and again served in Korea, where he may have been wounded.

Meeting, managing, and working with men whose mission and self-respect was more important than self-preservation was an inspiration to me. Indeed, they faced danger daily; I faced it infrequently. They dealt with personal deprivation continually; I experienced it minimally by comparison and played out my tour in only slightly uncomfortable conditions.

I performed surgery in a semi-protected environment, following which I could wander off to my bunk and lie down. By contrast, between firefights they would call a hole in the ground home. When brought in to us injured, their demeanor was that of frustration and determination, hardly defeat.

What made Vietnam so vicious is that the enemy felt the same way. The Viet Cong were an able foe, and the men serving the cause were as dedicated to winning as our marines were. That made for some tough fighting for both sides.

In the middle of a hot, clear July day, I got a firsthand view of the Viet Cong's determination to achieve victory. As usual, a Huey roared in to the landing pad, and we all rushed toward the shock tent. What struck me as odd, though, was that there was only one casualty, and he was Vietnamese. Usually there would have been more casualties. While we treated mostly Americans, we did treat South Vietnamese soldiers and civilians, as well. A short time later, another helicopter descended upon us with no casualties at all, and I began to wonder what was going on. Two marine officers from the intelligence section at the marine division headquarters somewhere near Da Nang stepped off this craft.

It turned out that this particular casualty was not just a Vietnamese but was a member of the Viet Cong, our enemy, who had been injured in battle. Captured by the marines, he was brought to our surgical facility for care. He had an arm injury and a penetrating injury of the brain, thus mandating evacuation to a surgical facility capable of providing neurosurgical management. After evaluation we took him to the OR and prepared to operate. The chief of surgery then came and instructed me that the intelligence people wanted to interrogate this prisoner before he underwent cranial surgery.

My first thought was that they had no confidence in me and were concerned he would be much worse off following the surgery. In fact, however, I was more experienced in this time frame. I conjectured that they thought it wise to gain as much information as possible beforehand. I was more confident in my ability than they were, but it was their call. I acquiesced and simply stood by the patient on the operating table, waiting in a semi-interested way as they questioned this young man. He appeared to be about eighteen or nineteen years old. He was dressed in the typical civilian attire of the Vietnamese, not much. No other component of a uniform was present to suggest that he was a member of armed forces. The boy was able to talk rather clearly in his native tongue to an interpreter provided by marines. One of the intelligence officers asked him various technical questions, for which he gave some answers and refused to respond to others. This seemed rather routine to me.

At the end of the interrogation, the intelligence officer asked, through the interpreter, "Why do you fight for the Communist forces?" The young prisoner responded (again through the interpreter) that he was convinced that their cause was entirely appropriate, and that the non-Communist forces were entirely in error. He went on to say that if he could return to his colleagues in arms, he would again take up the fight against the American forces.

I was surprised and wondered about his remarks. Is he fully aware of his predicament? Not only was the young man in the hands of his enemy, who might react to this assertion with more than a passing interest, of more concern he surely was aware he was about to undergo surgery by members of his enemy who could harm or kill him. Evidently, this was a very courageous young man fully committed to a cause. He had strongly bonded with the Viet Cong and its political agenda.

The surgery was completed uneventfully. He improved and then was turned over to the South Vietnamese forces as a prisoner of war. For several days afterward, I reflected on his remarks and his strength of resolve, which possibly was being reinforced by the antimilitary attitude of some of the American populace and even many of our politicians.

I wondered further how many of his colleagues held the same iron mind-set of passion motivating them to inflict more and more casualties on American troops. I was too busy and committed to patient care to think about the developing opposition to the war back home. My personal opinion of the war was not crystallized until I returned to the United States and followed the media. At that point I became hostile towered the protesting element. Curiously, one year later and more informed, I agreed that the war was a mistake.

On our officer staff there was a security commander in charge of a platoon of about fifty marines stationed at the hospital, whose function it was to provide protection of the hospital compound, hospital staff, and patients. He advised all personnel, physicians, medical administrative people, and the corpsmen on matters of security. Included in his recommendations was the advice to dig a foxhole near one's rack that he could scramble to in the event of mortar attack and overrun.

Curiously, the response to his recommendation was variable. The range of interest varied from no compliance to deep holes dug in the sand in the recommended areas. The average individual did dig a hole about four to five feet deep and about four square feet. The soil was generally sandy, so the effort was not overwhelming for any of us. Mine was approximately these dimensions and was dug the same day I was advised to do so, which meant right after I arrived at China Beach in January.

Because of the sandy soil, the foxholes required regular maintenance. I faithfully carried it out, as needed, borrowing a shovel from the Sea Bees and digging the hole to the proper dimensions. One bright summer day, I was shoveling out my foxhole to deepen it slightly and enlarge its width. In a sense, the work represented a diversion, and I enjoyed the distraction. Jerry Long, the acknowledged academician of the medical officer complement of the hospital, wandered by and stopped to talk and to offer advice as I worked.

"How deep are you going to dig that hole, Paul?" he asked. "Looks plenty deep enough to me."

"I'm digging my way through to the other side of the world," I said. "To the Midwest, where it's cooler."

"Dig faster," Long said. "I'm coming with you!"

We laughed at that and exchanged some more small talk before the conversation shifted from the superficial to the more esoteric, specifically to a scientific agenda. Injuries of the brain created by penetrating missiles were and still are distinctly unusual in most hospital settings. He, like me, was well aware that we were in a unique environment in that we had a large complement of head-injury patients in our hospital at any one time, and he suggested that there might be a possibility of deriving scientific information from certain chemical imbalances in their blood. He went on to say that if we could identify that imbalance, then the information might be helpful in caring for this uncommon type of injury.

"The only imbalance is the loss of blood," I said, having stopped my shoveling to engage Jerry more seriously. "I really don't think there would be a chemical difference in the blood of a patient with a head injury compared to the blood of a patient with another type of wound. Why would there be?"

"We won't know unless we investigate!" Jerry said.

While I continued to dig and think, he stood and thought (hardly a balanced effort) about what sort of study we might carry out. He ultimately suggested (and I agreed) that the serum of blood maintained at the certain osmotic equilibrium in the bodies of all might possibly undergo temporary changes in all injured individuals, and might quite likely undergo an even further alteration in individuals with head injuries.

A short time later, we began collecting blood samples for the study. We were strongly motivated by the fact that never again (we hoped) would there be a chance to carry out such a scientific study. You'd need a war to generate that many head-injury cases over a long period of time, and, sadly, we had an increasingly vicious war on our hands. Later, we compiled the data and published a paper in a medical journal after our tours of duty in Vietnam ended and we returned to naval duty in the United States.

In the interest of surgical progress, I bring to awareness an issue that troubled me at this point in my Vietnam tour.

Bullets impact the brain by piercing the scalp and rigid skull before entering the brain. In doing so the bullet proceeds on a straight course and tiny fragments of the skull also are flung into the brain. These unlike the bullet scatter wide in brain substance.

Studies by a neurosurgical investigator during the Korean War concluded that these bone chips cause dangerous infection unless deftly removed. To achieve this, a surgeon is forced to carry the surgery to further locations in the brain damaging additional brain.

I was skeptical and became involved in researching this matter when I returned to a naval hospital stateside. Our conclusions implied that bone chip removal was not necessary and other investigators agreed. (Addendum)

Bone chip removal is no longer a firm policy.

While I took care of my foxhole, I did not go overboard. However, one of my colleagues really took the plunge. He arrived at the height of summer as the replacement for our orthopedic surgeon who had rotated back home. The new guy's name was Al Johnson. Dr. Johnson—or Al, as we officers called him—was an outgoing, pleasant physician of medium size who demonstrated a remarkable potential to gain weight even on the often-disappointing chow we ate. He had dark hair neatly combed to the right, round appealing dark eyes, and a most friendly manner. His jungle uniform was appropriately pressed and clean, as was his cover. He walked with an energetic bounce, as if he was eager to get to his destination.

Since Al was brand-new to Vietnam and probably had heard a great deal about the ghastly ramifications of war, he had a healthy respect for personal safety. Accordingly, he wore his weapon constantly and, for all I know, even had it on his bunk at night. What was apparent to all of us, and as further evidence that he had a fearful respect for the enemy and its lethal power, was the fact that Al very promptly proceeded to dig his foxhole directly adjacent to his Quonset hut. This did not seem out of the ordinary, except it became the most elaborate structure of its kind I ever saw in Vietnam.

It was at least eight feet deep and about twelve feet wide. Not only was it a hole, but in addition he procured sections of metal landing matting. Several of these he stretched across the top of his foxhole (or, I should say, "protection chamber") to provide a roof-like structure, on top of which he shoveled at least a two-foot-thick veneer of the sandy surface.

The entrance to this cave-like edifice was through a sloping, slender entry that he carved on one corner of the deep hole. To enter, one was required to slither either headfirst or feetfirst down a forty-five-degree slope into the hole directly under the landing matting–covered sandy roof and into a black abyss.

We all marveled at this architectural masterpiece and echoed our compliments to him. Al's jovial ego was not the least bit offended; in fact, I believe he enjoyed the adulation and frivolity directed his way. Indeed, from our perspective, not only would he be protected from exploding mortar rounds but possibly could take a direct hit (something we could not). In addition, since the surrounding area was a sandy surface, any overrunning enemy infantry might completely miss the foxhole, even possibly running over the top. To be sure, the sloping entrance on one end was not particularly obvious to an individual who would rush by in a hurry, especially in the twilight or after dark.

It was acknowledged that Al had, by anyone's estimate, the most secure foxhole on the hospital compound and quite possibly anywhere in Vietnam. It had one flaw, however, which none of us anticipated. During the daylight hours the navy would allow Vietnamese women to come into the compound to work as maids, including keeping the officers' quarters.

As fate would have it, these women assumed that Dr. Johnson's foxhole was, in fact, a glorified latrine and would routinely slide into the entrance and both defecate and urinate in this majestic mausoleum.

Despite every effort by Dr. Johnson, and I suspect a recommendation from someone in administration, these poor women could not understand that this structure was designed for any reason other than a lavatory strictly for their use.

Several times during my tour of Vietnam, the attack siren sent me jumping into my foxhole. After learning of the use to which the Vietnamese women had put his masterpiece, I never dared ask Al if he personally used his edifice. However, aware of his extraordinary fear of the enemy, I suspect he did so on more than one occasion. His creation became known as "Fort Johnson."

About halfway through my tour in Vietnam, the first of two hospital ships, the USS *Repose*, arrived on station and announced that its medical team would begin accepting casualties. Among the surgeons were the usual emergency specialties, such as general surgery, orthopedics, and neurosurgery. In addition, the ship carried subspecialties, such as urology, ophthalmology, and otolaryngology.

The ship was large enough to handle one thousand patients at a time, or about three to four times the capacity of the average community hospital. These floating hospitals functioned with a ship's component of sailors to operate the vessel, and a full medical component—physicians, medical administrators, nurses, and corpsmen—to care for patients. The ship had operating rooms, X-ray facilities, intensive care units, general medical and surgical units, and any other ancillary medical services that would be found in a stateside hospital.

Once the command indicated that the medical facilities were fully operational, casualty-carrying helicopters often vectored to the ship, in addition to China Beach, and to the three marine field hospitals: A, B, and Charlie Med. The new medical capacity was a welcome and helpful addition. We were bending under the strain of casualty numbers and were more than moderately relieved to have the assistance.

There were unfortunately a couple of negative aspects of the hospital ship. The fact that it would steam continually back and forth from north to south while about twenty miles offshore, thus changing its position constantly relative to our facility, made finding it an issue in foul weather or at night.

Its navigational system for incoming helicopters was a bit less than that offered at land-based fields. This forced the pilot to rely upon visual aids in locating the vessel.

I recall one night about midnight during a very heavy rain, an evacuation helicopter arrived at our compound with a battle casualty. It was a head injury. I was in the operating room at the time and probably would have been tied up for another two hours. I advised a member of the hospital administration that the helicopter take this casualty out to the hospital ship. The pilots agreed and headed out to sea. Apparently over land they usually navigated in the region around Da Nang by simply recognizing the hills and valleys that they had flown over so often. They would stay within two hundred and four hundred feet above ground and find our facility in any weather with no difficulty.

Once they began to fly over the ocean, however, all landmarks were lost, and with the heavy rain, visibility in the distance was down to less than half a mile. Thus, visual recognition of the ship was not possible, and the navigational signals echoed by aircraft carriers and airfields to incoming aircraft were not available.

After one hour of searching, the pilot abruptly reversed his course, returned to us, and deposited the casualty, stating that further efforts to find the vessel were futile and quite dangerous. Thus, in inclement weather and at night, China Beach again became the only locus of neurosurgical support.

This did not represent an excess burden since we had become so accustomed to meeting this responsibility. However, it was disappointing that we were only transiently augmented in many facets of medicine and surgery.

An additional undesirable feature was the reality that after a few months on station, the ship would steam back to the Philippines, where the hospital crew could get rest and relaxation while the vessel was resupplied and refueled.

At this time, August 1966, I had profited from many months of surgical experience, plus a plethora of both gratifying and depressing emotions. Such translated into an enhanced image of myself as both a man and a surgeon. The CO knew how hard I'd been working, and he came up to me one morning and said, "Pitlyk! Take a break and go out to the hospital ship for lunch."

Impressed that he thought of me, I said thanks. A Huey

came in, and I hopped on. Off we went, twenty miles out to sea, sweeping relatively low across the water. I could see the ship about six to eight miles in the distance, silhouetted brilliantly against the greenish turquoise of the South China Sea. The ship itself was painted stark white and displayed a large red cross on the side of her bow. She carved a slender white wake through the water, and from the air the combination of the turquoise ocean, the ultra-blue sky, the striking white vessel, and the long slender foam-white wake was a sight to behold.

We landed quickly on the landing pad at the stern. I was met and treated to a quick tour of the ship by the neurosurgeon dressed in the bright white of a naval officer's summer uniform. He was Bill Sanders, graduate of Syracuse University who would return there as a professor of neurosurgery after his time in the navy. He treated me to lunch in the officers' ward room with its linen white tablecloths, most suitable tasty food, and engaging company. All this in aggregate presented a most pleasant ambience.

A sense of embarrassment taunted me, dressed as I was in the drab khaki field uniform, including heavy dusty boots while everyone else on board was attired in impeccable white uniforms.

After lunch, we walked up on the upper decks and again were treated to marvelous ocean views. A few moments later we heard the thundering roar of a jet engine, and in an instant an American Navy attack bomber, apparently returning from a mission, flew about three hundred feet above the water along one side of the ship. He then did a couple of barrel rolls, following which he angled the plane upward and seemingly disappeared into the brilliant blue sky.

We then went to the ship's interior, where I had a chance to view enviously, to say the least, the operating rooms replete with modern equipment, and the intensive care unit with its spotless floors and neat linen sheets. It was a quite professional atmosphere free of sand. We then toured the wards and again were met with an equally quite professional, spotlessly clean area. Included were bed racks formed from what looked like doors hinged to the wall parallel to the floor and suspended on the other (unhinged side) by chain attached to the bulkhead. The bed arrangement was much like many drawbridges that had been lowered.

Scurrying about I saw nurses in starched white uniforms, looking both attractive and efficient. I had forgotten what a modern hospital looked like. After two hours, I was advised that our helicopter was getting ready to return to Da Nang. I said good-bye to my charming hosts, pulled on my flight helmet, climbed inside the olive-drab helicopter, strapped my safety belt tight, and then felt the vibration of the straining engine and watched as the ship slowly disappeared below us. Again, it stood out as a beautiful white marble monument in the incredible background of an otherwise pristine sea.

The craft headed toward Da Nang, and in less than thirty minutes we descended toward and landed on the tarmac of our hospital, where I was again greeted with the whirling sand and gravel and dreary assemblage of Quonset huts.

At that moment I felt the gritty sensation of sand in my mouth and knew I was home again.

Hospital ship off coast of Da Nang in South China Sea

17
MISSION OF MERCY

IN CENTRAL DA NANG, SIX MILES from China Beach, there was a civilian hospital where patients were desperately in need of care. I learned about the US Overseas Mission Hospital from one of my administrators, who told me conditions there were about as bad as they could get.

"How bad could it be?" I asked, not fully realizing the importance of my question.

The administrator looked at me, his eyes sad. "You've got to see it to believe it, sir! It's beyond anything you could ever imagine."

I doubted that, but I said nothing while the administrator informed me that the only medical care for the people was from volunteer Vietnamese nurses, a half dozen or so American nurses, and whatever military doctors from the American forces were willing to lend a hand. Navy policy stipulated that physicians at China Beach could attend and manage patients at the USOM Hospital when they were not encumbered with marine casualties. He said if I wanted to help, I would always be provided with a jeep, a driver, and prompt radio communication to the hospital so that if casualties arrived at our facility I could immediately return to base.

"Okay, then," I said. "I'll go take a look."

"Thanks, Doc," he said. "They really need guys like you to pitch in."

I procured a jeep from our motor pool and drove into Da Nang with the administrator, who knew the location of the hospital. We encountered the usual marine checkpoints, but the troopers passed us through. The unpaved streets of Da Nang were narrow and congested, and they were lined with one- and two-story stucco, old, dirty, French buildings. Puddles of human waste steeped everywhere in the heat, and the odor as we drove was a combination of thick diesel exhaust, excrement, and urine. The plumbing in Da Nang was very limited, so sewage got dumped out windows. The people were dressed in light, worn cotton garments, badly in need of washing. Women were the bearers of goods, such as fish and vegetables, which were held in twin wicker baskets balanced over the shoulder by a wood pole about five feet long.

We arrived at our destination, another old, stucco, dirty, French two-story building. As we walked into the medium-sized two-door main entrance from an unpaved adjacent parking area, we entered an atrium with old cracked marble floors thoroughly soaked with a variety of human fluids, and stained a yellow brown. There were plaster walls, dark yellow in color, which were quite dirty and had cracks throughout. On the left side of the atrium was a stairwell constructed of old broken mosaic-like marble steps. These stairs led to a second-floor dormitory-like area functioning as the hospital ward.

When I walked into the ward, the odor of feces, vomit, and infection was most intense. Flies were legion. This relatively large room had about a fifteen-foot ceiling and several window frames along the walls, none of which had windowpanes or screens. Old, poorly kept hospital beds with no mattresses, only the typical single cross-wired bed frames, were available for patient use. All the sixty beds were jammed side by side such that an attendant could barely walk between them. Various assortments of tattered cloth and occasionally torn linoleum were stretched over the bedsprings, on top of which was not one but routinely two patients per single bed.

I was quite frankly appalled at what I saw, and I agreed to help in whatever way I could. I had been in Vietnam for months at this point, and I told myself that I should not have been moved by what I saw, but I still was.

It was common for all sixty beds in the hospital to be full, with two patients on each. The overflow patients were forced to remain on the old contaminated cracked marble floor, either crouched in a corner or propped up on the floor against a sidewall. Flies swarmed continuously.

Usually a family member would be present with some sort of food for the patients since this was not provided by the hospital. I recall frequently seeing a small gallon-sized pail filled about three-quarters of the way with a thin soup-like material in which small fish, head included, were floating on the surface. I often heard patients calling out for "Nuc-Bom." I learned that this was a common seasoning sprinkled on their rice, a major food staple for the people in this region and throughout Vietnam.

Most of the patients were victims of trauma. Obviously, war had no respect for the non-aggressor. It was common to walk into this ward and see patients with recently amputated legs above or below the knee and with the operative site wrapped with a dirty blood-soaked linen while flies crawled on the dressing. Similar injuries to the arms were numerous.

Less commonly, patients would be lying there with untreated abdominal, chest, or head wounds simply because with such injuries, their lives were abbreviated. Again, flies were constantly present, crawling on the blood-soaked dressings, milling about the soup, and often seen floating in it. Flies were even in the operating rooms, which also had unprotected window apertures. Plumbing was minimal. The few toilets were overflowing or out of commission. Electric power was available yet subject to blackouts.

There were some Vietnamese nurses who made a reasonable effort to keep the patients clean; however, the numerical superiority of victims-to-a-nurse ratio simply overwhelmed these women. Additionally, the nurses were like most of the civilians, poorly educated and quite superstitious. For instance, if a patient died in the hospital, it was assumed that the "Death Spirit" was in the building and would be there for several hours. Therefore, all patient relatives and patients who could walk, in addition to all the Vietnamese nurses, would depart from the building and not return for several hours. During such a hiatus, patients survived with the care provided by the handful of American nurses.

The main floor housed the receiving room or emergency area and three operating rooms. The operating rooms were the size of a small kitchen and had the now-familiar old cracked tile floor and stucco walls that were dirty, stained, and cracked. Single windows faced the exterior, but they were absent of panes. Someone had leaned a screen against the OR windows to keep the flies out of the surgical area; however, it did not work. The overhead operating lights were of marginal quality yet were acceptable. The operating table was an old device that I am sure exceeded seventy years of age. It had mechanical cranks to change it into different positions for various types of procedures. Such might still be seen in a museum of medicine in the United States.

Operating supplies and instruments were quite austere. Indeed, much of the time the navy physicians would bring surgical instruments and anesthesia gas containers with them to do an operation.

The one factor that rendered this facility reasonably acceptable by American physician standards was the presence of the seven American volunteer nonmilitary nurses who presumably had agreed to work at the facility for an extended period of time. They spoke our language, were American trained, and fortunately had a high frustration threshold.

Outside the main entrance and across the gravel- and dirt-covered parking area was a single-level pavilion-like structure built directly on the soil. It had a thatched gabled roof and vertical four-by-fours supporting the same. There was about a four-foot-high wall made of wood surrounding the structure, above which was exposure to the elements. This was the Vietnamese equivalent of a rehabilitation center into which food was brought for the patients by family or friends. This building had no plumbing, water, or electric lights. The single advantage of this structure over the hospital was that the stench was not nearly as intense, thanks to the fact that there were no enclosing walls and, thus, there was a rapid exchange of air in and out of the structure.

The emergency room was attached to the main building just beyond the operating area and had an open door looking out over an unpaved parking area. Into this flowed patients conveyed by transportation such as run-down vehicles or stretchers. Between these extremes of conveyance were wooden wagons or crude wooden wheelbarrows. Some people actually crawled in.

The emergency room consisted of a receiving section just beyond the entrance, which, like other rooms in this old French building, had a cracked tile or marble floor usually contaminated with soil, dried blood, urine, and occasionally feces. The plaster walls were cracked and failing. There was an overhead ceiling light with a single bare lightbulb hanging from a light socket connected across the ceiling and down the side wall by a black snakelike cord stapled to the wall. Air-conditioning was out of the question.

This admitting area served as a semi-processing room where identification was confirmed and some sort of a chart was assembled, following which the patient was ushered into the medical emergency area. This was a longer, somewhat narrow corridor-like room similar to other rooms in the building.

This long narrow area was furnished with about fourteen old gurneys arranged in a parallel order along one wall. Activity was continuous, noisy, seemingly chaotic, and charged with tension. The familiar flies were well represented, and the overwhelming stench was ever present. The grounds around the hospital were not paved. It was dust in the dry season and mud during the rainy periods.

I began working when I was available. My work consisted of neurosurgical cases. Often my able assistant, Bart, accompanied me. One day when he was with me exemplified what the Vietnamese civilians went through as a matter of course. Since no Vietnamese doctors attended the hospital, Bart and I were busy.

On this day we went over to the emergency room, evidently to answer a call for a severe head injury. We could barely move because the gurneys were so close together, but we found our patient, who happened to be a third of the way down the line from the entrance.

We went up to him quickly and observed that he was

bleeding badly from a severe gash of his scalp, which was probably fourteen inches long. The scalp was hanging backward from the irregular jagged laceration originating just above his right ear, advancing forward onto his forehead just in front of his hairline, across the forehead to the opposite side, and back to the left ear. The laceration was such that the scalp was literally hanging backward via gravity as he lay on the gurney. He was nearly scalped. Exposed was his bleeding bony skull now covered with dirt, debris, and a myriad of crawling flies.

Recognizing after my gross evaluation that the patient had not sustained an injury of the brain itself but rather only a major laceration of the scalp, Bart and I went about arranging to close this nasty laceration right there on the gurney rather than to tie up an operating room.

At the same time, the gurney on our patient's right harbored a patient who had a shattered right leg just below his knees, such that the leg was angulated ninety degrees and bone material was sticking out through his skin, from which was draining blood sprinkled with dirt. Again droves of flies! He had not been given analgesic medication and was both moaning continuously and writhing in pain.

On the other side of our patient's gurney was a young woman in the process of delivering a baby right on the gurney. A quick look confirmed that the baby's head was already out of the vagina. The woman also had not yet been given any form of the analgesic. It is quite possible none was available for her. The flies greeted her newborn baby by lounging about on its exposed head.

At that moment, Bart turned to me and said, "Doctor, this is enough to make the pope curse." He was dispassionate and marvelous. You could not get him down.

The injuries at the USOM Hospital were much like those seen at China Beach. The anesthetist at the civilian hospital fortunately was one of the American nurses who had training in anesthesia and did an impressive job in spite of the equipment she was obligated to work with at the facility she was working in. Fortunately I had Bart to assist me at surgery. He was prepared to break away from the operating table and fix failing equipment at any time such might, and often did, occur.

On one occasion, I was operating on a patient when the ever-important suction device, which we used to clear blood from the operating field so that we can work our way about either a brain or the spinal canal, suddenly failed. In the stateside hospital, and even in this primitive place, some sort of suction equipment was connected to a vacuum line originating from outside one wall of the operating room to which we could connect a sterile piece of rubber tubing and a small metal suction catheter. With this I could continually aspirate and remove blood and debris from the operating field, thus facilitating my dissection. I cannot overemphasize how important this suction equipment is to not only a neurosurgeon but to all surgeons in the course of an operative procedure.

During this operation, the suction tube suddenly failed. Blood began to accumulate in the operative field, and I could not navigate through the tissue planes. I promptly turned around and looked at the suction tubing that I held in my hand and then followed its course with my eyes downward, across the floor, and to the wall where the suction source was located. I noticed that the old rubber tubing had simply fallen apart in its course across the floor.

I quickly asked one of the Vietnamese nurses in the room to "fix it." It obviously required a small rigid metal, plastic, or glass connector to connect the two separated ends of the hose and, thus, reestablish suction. Her response to my request was to simply reconnect the tubing with a small solid wooden dowel that she picked up from somewhere in the room. This, indeed, reconstituted the tubing but in no way reestablished the suction mechanism.

Fortunately, Bart saw as quickly as I did that this young woman had no concept of our needs and left the operating table, took off his operating gloves, found a hollow piece of tubing, reconnected the two severed sections of the rubber tubing, and reestablished my suction system. He then quickly washed his hands.

"I only have time to kill the germs, LT! Can't wait around for the funeral!" he shouted as he yanked on a clean set of gloves and returned to my side.

On another occasion, a Vietnamese woman was shown to me with a large pulsating mass on the left side of her neck just below the angle of her jaw. The skin overlying the mass was macerated and beginning to indicate necroses (dying). I looked at the lesion, palpated it, and recognized immediately that it was probably a large traumatic aneurysm of her left carotid artery that probably had been caused by a penetrating injury to her neck.

Following such, the damaged wall of the artery began to balloon out under the arterial pressure to cause this Ping-Pong ball–sized dome to protrude from the side of her neck. The mass then brought about pressure on the overlying skin and it turned black and blue and began to decay. The lesion was now on the verge of literally exploding. This would release her blood under pressure to the exterior, and she would promptly die.

It was my plan to return the next day with a general surgeon and carry out the surgery necessary to correct this problem, but for the next four days I was delayed by surgery at our place. When I returned to the USOM, I asked to see this woman and was advised that the night before, while sleeping in the ward, there was observed by other patients a sudden gush of blood from the side of her neck that sprayed almost ten feet across three of four beds adjacent to her. She writhed briefly and then died.

As if the entire scene was not routinely surreal and sad enough, I learned that the Viet Cong had become aware that the American Navy had a doctor who operated on the head, and they therefore began to use us as a referral service. It was not uncommon to find two or three relatively young Vietnamese men with penetrating head injuries lying on the front steps of the hospital early in the morning on various days.

The American nurses told me what the Viet Cong were up to: creeping onto the hospital grounds in the middle of the night, dropping off their head-injured wounded in the parking lot in front of the emergency room, and then scattering.

We, of course, were indiscriminate in our management of the native population and would carry out the necessary surgery and postoperative care, subsequent to which these same young men would disappear from the hospital, again in the middle of the night.

We carried out a cranial procedure on such a man who then convalesced on the second floor of the hospital, routinely sharing a single bed with another patient. He became quite verbose and argumentative. As he improved, he would jabber boisterously in an arrogant, mostly hostile fashion in his native tongue, remarking that he "had tricked the American doctors into operating" on his brain when, in fact, he "was a member of enemy forces bent on killing Americans."

It became apparent that he would save his verbal fusillade until I came in the hospital on certain days. He would then shout in a very animated fashion, again in his native tongue, how clever he was and how naive and foolish we were to literally play into the enemy's hands.

I always worked with an interpreter while making rounds in the hospital and became accustomed with this young man's obnoxious behavior. One day, I listened as he shouted away. Then I turned to the interpreter and said, "If he ever talks to me again, I'll have him put in a prison somewhere deep in the United States where he will languish until the day he dies."

Of course, I had absolutely no authority, and indeed if I had such, there was no intent to do such a thing. However, it worked. He became quiet and subdued, remaining a model patient for the subsequent days that he was treated at the USOM Hospital. Like the rest of his Viet Cong comrades, he disappeared one evening and I suspect made his way back into the enemy lines to again do battle with our marines.

I did a lot of surgery there with Bart as my steadfast assistant. He was eager to help and was very good. With time he became familiar with the principles and necessary surgical moves. It was a good thing because one day we were in the middle of an operation at USOM when China Beach called with a head-injured marine. I was forced to turn the operation over to Bart and leave to go back to our home base. You should have seen the terrified look on his face when I said, "Bart, take over!" Thanks to his ability, the patient recovered. I recall afterward telling Bart I was going to turn him in for practicing medicine without a license.

Many others from China Beach—including surgeons, occasionally anesthesiologists, internists, and general medical officers—spent many hours and many days in this run-down hospital during our tour of duty. Many dozens—or, more probably, hundreds—of Vietnamese civilians, along with the enemy, benefited from this altruistic gesture of the US Navy.

To what extent this effort, if at all, improved the image of the Americans in the eyes of the Vietnamese people remains an enigma. However, even though our help was facilitated by the US government for possibly political an self-saving reasons, the individual efforts by the physicians, corpsmen, and so many other navy personnel were based entirely on compassion toward fellow man.

That the USOM Hospital ran as effectively and as efficiently as it did was exclusively the result of those few American nurses providing training and support to the Vietnamese personnel. These women carved one or two years out of their lives to exist in an abominable environment by anyone's standards in an effort to make a positive impact on people victimized by war. Over the many years since I last saw any of them, I occasionally wonder what became of these ladies. Did they become victims of the same conflict they had volunteered to become entangled in, or had they rotated after their tour of duty back to the United States and reentered a more rational lifestyle?

What motivated them to go there in the first place and endure the incredible deprivation of not only the lack of aesthetics of day-to-day life, but the vexing and seemingly insurmountable odds of providing even marginal standard of care for those poor wretched people? This baffled me then and continues to do so.

I do not remember any of their names, nor can I recall their faces; however, I will never forget what they did. Like the marines, they were true heroes.

Volunteering at the USOM Hospital was not without its risks. As much as 30 percent or more of the population of Da Nang was sympathetic to the Viet Cong. Enemy soldiers lived in the city, and they moved freely about because they were able to blend in with the civilians. You never knew if you were talking to an enemy combatant, and it was unnerving.

If an American ran across the wrong guy, or group of guys, death was a distinct possibility. Still, I became complacent after many months of driving to and from the hospital. I didn't even take a driver with me all the time and Bart could not always be available.

On one typical summer day, I finished my rounds and then got a jeep and headed out of China Beach at around ten in the morning. The sky was bright and clear, and although it was hot, the weather was not unpleasant. I drove out of the gates beyond the marine guards and proceeded down the road through the various checkpoints, traversing the pontoon bridge of the Da Nang River with the now-familiar riflemen firing away at lily pads that might be concealing explosive gifts from the Viet Cong.

Soon I was on the familiar semi-maintained narrow streets of Da Nang, headed toward the downtown area. As I drove along I saw groups of Vietnamese civilians, many of whom shouldered goods of one type or another in the familiar wicker baskets suspended on either end of bamboo poles. Other individuals were simply standing about talking. Some were children.

The traffic slowed to about ten miles an hour due to the civilian population walking in each direction on the barely allowable two-lane street congested with both military vehicles and some foreign civilian vehicles. The vehicles were working their way between the people who not infrequently would walk almost in the center of the roadway, fully realizing they were halting traffic. I was familiar with this methodical slow mode of traffic and paid little attention to it.

Soon congestion began to thin out, and I was able to move somewhat faster. Suddenly, I was struck in the head by a golf ball–size rock thrown from my left from somewhere in the crowd. I was momentarily stunned, but I did not lose consciousness and I certainly did not lose control of the vehicle. I looked out the left side of the jeep and saw a group of Vietnamese men scattering in various directions. I am sure they were fearful that I would draw my weapon and begin firing vindictively into their midst. Recognizing that it was futile to track down the perpetrator, I simply guided the jeep, down the road, and continued on my trip to the hospital.

The incident shook me up a little. I'd have died if that rock had been a hand grenade, and that feeling made me uneasy about traveling alone. I therefore subsequently avoided traveling alone.

Previously, I'd found the delays at marine checkpoints frustrating and downright annoying, but after that encounter with a faceless Viet Cong member, I changed. The many stern marines barking blunt unanimated questions at checkpoints were as common as booming artillery in the distance, and I was glad they were around.

Patient ward USOM Hospital Da Nang

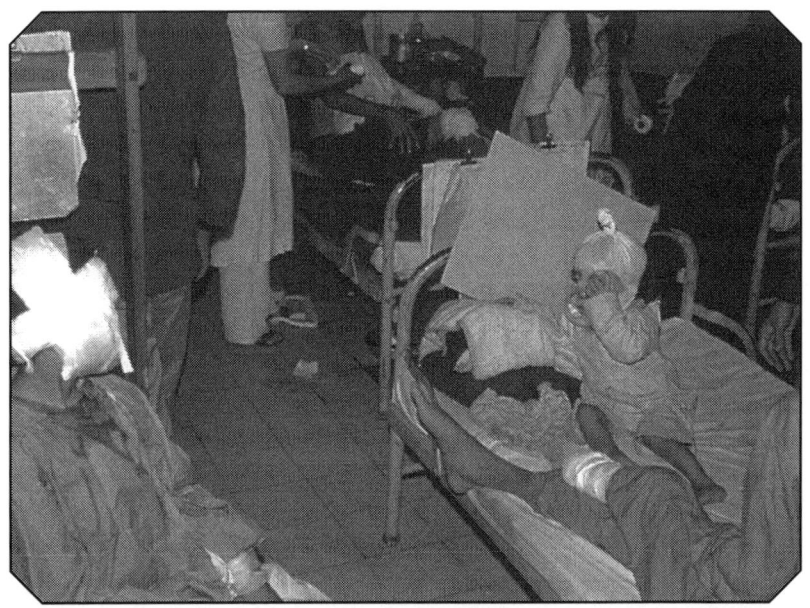

Injured patients hospitalized at USOM Hospital Da Nang

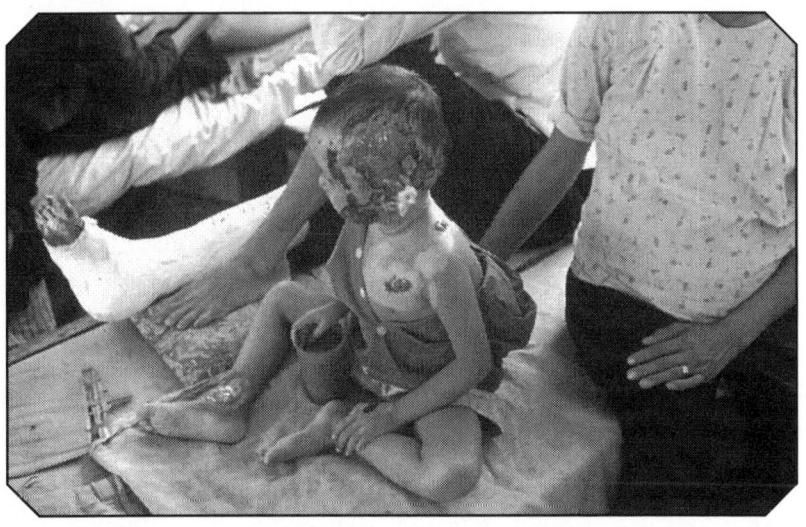

Injured Vietnamese child at USOM Hospital Da Nang

18

Winding Down

THE TUMULT AND BLOODSHED OF THE summer did not relent with the coming of autumn. If anything, the conflict in Vietnam had grown exponentially with the expanded American effort that led to the introduction of tens of thousands more men into the widening field of operations. Bombing runs, search-and-destroy missions, and the dislocation of the civilian population from the hot zones marked the slow passage of time. At China Beach, we felt the impact of the burgeoning war in the steadily increasing number of wounded brought in on the Hueys.

Yet, in many ways, the days and weeks sped ever faster toward the conclusion of my tour of duty. Strangely, I found myself torn between desiring the comforts of home and my desire to remain at China Beach, where I was making a tangible difference in the lives of many wounded marines. I still struggled with the hard questions that any combat doctor must face, but those questions weighed less heavily on me. I accepted the inevitable defeats, and I rejoiced in the victories I achieved on the operating table.

As previously noted, the brain contains many vital centers, and each of these is indeed a control center for specific life-sustaining functions. Additionally, there are speech organizing and controlling areas, an emotional controlling center, and the widely distributed cognitive center. This center, in many respects, can be considered the repository of our education and life experience from which we make intelligent decisions.

As neurosurgeons we must respect these critical areas and carry out surgical procedures peripheral to such centers. Regrettably the fragments hurled by exploding weapons of war don't care where they end up. They scatter throughout the brain. More often than I can recall, I found myself in situations where, in an effort to preserve the life of the patient, it was necessary to carry out surgical procedures that violated these crucial centers. Some marines died, some became vegetables, and a few recovered. Without question, we sometimes made decisions that only God had a right to make.

There were times when I was rewarded with a marvelous result. Clearly, that was the nature of my chosen field. Behind us we often left a trail of dead and crippled individuals. But there were successes even when a soldier had sustained a head injury of immense magnitude. I often had doubts about the outcome during surgery, and yet with a Herculean effort the battle was won. The patient not only survived, but he did so with a full recovery of his normal mental functions.

It was in moments such as these that I would commonly reflect upon what my life would be like had I not joined the navy. I would still be in Milwaukee, evaluating people with less threatening injuries, and I'd have far fewer life-and-death situations. I would have been carrying out surgical operations of lesser magnitude and complexity. That would have been the price of living a more comfortable life in late

1965 through much of 1966. During those scattered periods of favorable elation triggered by a gratifying surgical result and patient recovery, I would make a comparison of these two scenarios, and with no hesitation in each case, I chose the Vietnam experience.

To arbitrarily choose the chaotic austere, intimidating, fatiguing, and anxiety-generating life in Vietnam was not what I believe the average surgeon (or even the average person) would seek. I therefore wondered whether I was a little crazy, or if I had a masochistic personality. For whatever reason, though, I was beginning to savor the life I led at China Beach, and I had qualms about giving it up.

Late in my tour of duty, my faithful assistant's time in Vietnam ran out. It was October, and as I stood with him, waiting at the front gate for his transportation to the airfield, I pictured fall in the Midwest. I felt a pull toward home, a sort of manifestation of my ambivalence. For Bart's part, he couldn't wait to get back, and I understood why. Bart and I had been so talkative when we worked together, but we were each awkwardly looking for the right words to say good-bye.

Of course, there was no need to. The English language is not adequate to express what was between us. Bart was not a doctor or an officer, and he definitely was not a favorite of the CO, because he had too many shenanigans to his credit. Yet, this teenager had made a stunning impact on the medical care of patients at China Beach and the USOM Hospital. He was at China Beach when I arrived in my insecure state of mind, and I guessed he had fought his own inner battles with fear and insecurity, as well. Now we were confident in our ability to deal with the world, and Bart was about to embark to prove it.

After Bart's truck pulled up, we shook hands.

"Good luck," I said.

Bart swallowed hard. His eyes had a look of sadness and excitement.

"Don't eat too much steak," I said.

"Sure, LT," he said. "It's been something."

"Yes," I said, "it has."

Then he jumped into the truck, and the truck pulled out. Bart waved at me and I waved back, and that was that. Good-byes were never easy for me, and they were especially difficult at China Beach. I always felt very alone when friends like Bart left. I walked slowly to the officers' club, bought myself a drink, and climbed up on the raised platform on the roof—the "oasis."

From this vantage one could stare out at the squat gray huts and the rolling sand dunes. The heat was less oppressive. Soon the monsoon season would be on us, and the patter of the rain would drum relentlessly on the tin roofs of the Quonset huts, reminding us of how far from home we really were, how transient life is, and how violent a war zone can be. I sat thinking about Bart for a long time, and the memories of our close relationship made me feel a little better.

Whenever I wanted to go downtown to the USOM Hospital in Da Nang to manage charity patients or carry out surgery, I had gone looking for Bart. He would go with me whenever he could, and he provided invaluable assistance. Although he was not supposed to leave the hospital without the CO's okay, he always went anyway. How he got away with it remained a mystery I did not try to solve. He possessed a marvelous command of language, which helped when we had to communicate with the Vietnamese. His eagerness to help and to be involved, coupled with his ability to talk to others as if he had known them for years, continued to benefit both of us.

Bart was admired and respected by the people who

worked at the civilian hospital, and of course he was popular at our military hospital too. In retrospect I have concluded that because he worked inside and outside the rule book, his life was twice as full as mine. For example, I was advised once that the nurses at the civilian hospital in Da Nang were going to have a party in a French villa in downtown Da Nang on a particular evening. I was told that Bart was most welcome.

The realities of military life are such that an officer can gain access to a vehicle and also justify leaving his compound, in our case the hospital after dark, if the reasons satisfied one's superiors. We thus had direct access to those who ran the motor pool and had influence over the vehicle acquisition. No such privilege was available to enlisted men.

On the night of the party, Bart and I conspired together to get him off base so that he could attend. The plan was that I would, in pretext, tell the motor pool representative that my surgical services were needed at the USOM in Da Nang, even though it was after dark. I would, of course, need a vehicle such as an ambulance, which was a closed vehicle and from which I would not appear so obvious and alone as in an open jeep. It also had a large cross on the side, which hopefully would deflect any hostility from the Viet Cong. They frequented Da Nang after dark!

I was advised to take an armed guard for protection; however, I declined, stating that I was carrying my personal weapon and, secondly, the large darkened ambulance might persuade aggressors into thinking there were several personnel inside. The motor pool officer believed me, and I was given the ambulance to go to Da Nang.

I got in the vehicle, drove it away from the motor pool Quonset, circled around a dark Quonset to ensure I was not being watched, and then slowly drove about the landing pad and behind the shock tent, where Bart was hiding in a large trash can. As I pulled adjacent to the trash can, he leaped out, opened the back door of the ambulance, slid in under one of the stretchers inside, and slammed the door.

I then proceeded toward the main gate, which of course was manned by two marines. I presented them with a pass that had been given to me by the motor pool attendant. Then, as is customary, they flashed their flashlights in a cursory fashion inside the ambulance and toward the back. They did not see Bart, because he was hiding under one of the stretchers directly on the floor.

They passed me through. We then gleefully proceeded down the road toward Da Nang and through two checkpoints, laughing, joking, and complimenting ourselves on how we pulled one off.

We worked our way gradually into Da Nang and ultimately found the old French villa where indeed a most noisy and impressive party was taking place on the second floor. We hid the ambulance as well as possible in the dark narrow street and proceeded to the villa.

The door opened into an old, cracked, dusty marble floor to a rickety old staircase, beyond the atrium of the entrance. Up we went to the top of the stairs, opening into two or three larger rooms where there were at least forty people (all Americans), including many navy officers, plus all seven of the American nurses from the USOM Hospital and now Bart and me.

Someone had provided liquor and even a few (pseudo) hors d'oeuvres. It took Bart about twenty seconds to engage one of the nurses in conversation, whereas I was fumbling for words to acknowledge my presence. We milled about, enjoying ourselves for about an hour, when someone shouted, "Look out, the MPs are coming." We were strictly off-limits and in violation of navy regulations, so nobody was surprised the military police had decided to crash the party.

Indeed, we heard tramping of feet coming up the stairwell to the second floor. Again, the military officers might be able to avoid punishment if caught in this predicament, whereas an enlisted individual would promptly be hauled off to the local brig. Bart, therefore, ducked out on the second-floor back porch, hung on the gutter, and hand-walked his way from the porch so he would not be in the line of sight should one of the MPs walk out and look about the porch.

I stood in the doorway, hoping that I could persuade an MP to not even go out on the porch. They walked among the officers, looking at their identification papers and, of course their rank, and openly criticized our presence. So what! They then walked toward me and the porch; however, recognizing my doctor's insignia they were satisfied that I was not hiding someone beyond the doorway to the porch. Devious joker that I was! Thus, they chose to ignore the back porch and of course did not see Bart. They scowled that we were off-limits but concluded we were no threat to the war effort. Then they turned and tramped out.

Meanwhile, Bart was still hanging on the gutter, his knuckles getting whiter and whiter and his fingertips going numb. I leaned out, looked at him, and quipped, "They're still here, 'enlisted scum.'"

He said, "I can't last much longer!"

"Well, I'll just have one quick drink and then hopefully they will be gone."

So I wandered off, got another drink, came back out, and said, "Bart, they're gone."

He was greatly relieved as I helped him back on the porch. I looked at his fingers, which were cramped in a semi-flexed position, and indeed his knuckles were white. We shared my drink, and he quickly regained his gregarious nature. After another thirty or forty minutes, the party broke up and we returned by ambulance to the hospital while Bart again hid in the back under one of the stretchers.

I explained to the marine guards at each of the checkpoints that I was returning from the civilian hospital, having operated on a desperately injured patient who, thanks to my efforts, will recover.

We arrived back to our hospital compound, got through the main gate in the same manipulative fashion by which we exited, and I again drove behind the shock tent adjacent to the trash can, whereupon Bart opened the rear door of the ambulance, jumped out, and disappeared behind the large trash can.

There was a distinct contrast in this young man between his impressive intelligence, creative capability, and human compassion on one hand, and the more primitive animal instincts of a teenager on the other. I considered it to be a curious symbiotic relationship between the superego and the id in one individual. I really believe that the words *depression, boredom, intransigence,* and *fatigue* did not exist in Bart's mind.

As our relationship developed, my confidence in his ability continued to increase. He would follow me on rounds in the intensive care unit, meet me in the shock Quonset to evaluate incoming casualties, and make sure that I had everything I needed to carry out the necessary surgical procedures for the various emergencies as they came in.

There was always a general medical officer assigned as the attending physician in the shock Quonset. His primary function was to complete initial evaluation of casualties and advise the appropriate surgeons. It was not at all uncommon that I would find myself in the middle of a three-hour craniotomy when I would hear the increasing crescendo of a helicopter engine coming my way.

Not infrequently the emergency room physician would rush over to my operating room and blurt out, "Be quick, I have another one for you!"

For chest, abdomen, pelvis, or arm and leg injuries, this never happened, because there were three or four surgeons and orthopedists assigned to the hospital. Never were all in the operating room at one time. Therefore, an experienced surgeon was also available to evaluate the patient in the shock tent. Such was not the case for the single neurosurgeon. These young doctors seemed to think every head-injury case was on the verge of death.

Bart recognized that this was a common problem for me, and from then on when we were in the operating room he arranged for another corpsman to pass instruments to me while he monitored the situation. When an incoming chopper was heard, he would quietly slip out of the operating room, work his way down to the shock tent, look rather disinterestedly over the shoulder of the evaluating physician, and then return to the OR and whisper in my ear one of two phrases—either "Take your time" or "Why don't you move right along."

Bart's diagnostic abilities for severity of a head injury routinely exceeded those of any of the emergency room physicians. He was aware of the confidence I placed in him, yet he never let it go to his head. He held a finely tuned element of humility and displayed a lighthearted attitude. He was not in the least bit self-centered. I can say without hesitation that he provided a source of psychotherapy or emotional equanimity for me during the most arduous, anxiety-ridden segment of my professional life. Not surprisingly, our association blended into friendship.

I could vicariously appreciate the sense of loss and abandon felt by his professor father back at Ohio State University when his son announced his intention to forego education and join the navy. It is regrettable, however, that Bart's father was not aware of the positive impact this uneducated, young, carefree teenager made on the operation of a naval hospital in Vietnam and that he undoubtedly contributed to the survival of scores of American and Vietnamese casualties.

I found myself smiling as I recalled sneaking Bart off the base for that party. I even chuckled about how happy he was and how quickly the nurses were drawn to him. I finished my drink and exhaled loudly.

"Good-bye, good friend," I said quietly. "Good-bye."

19

SEPARATION ANXIETY

THE CO GAVE ME THE NEWS I expected but did not want to receive. "Lieutenant Pitlyk, we should have your replacement here in three weeks."

Even though I knew it was coming, the fact that I had to leave hit me hard. I forced myself to stand up straight and look the man in the eye as I saluted and said, "Yes, sir!"

"Regulations, you know," the CO said. "Everybody's got to rotate out."

"Yes, sir!" I said.

"Okay, Pitlyk, go on. Get on out of here. I got work to do."

I smiled at the CO, turned, and left his office.

Outside, the air smelled like rain. And I heard the distant *thump, thump, thump* of choppers. The OR would soon be busy, and I found myself hoping that there would be a head injury so that I could focus on that instead of on having to go.

Although each of the neurological casualties were different and always challenging, I no longer felt threatened or at a loss as to what to do. I had been empowered by the strength of the extensive experience I gained at Charlie Med and at China Beach. Though it might sound like an inflated boast, I harbored the unmitigated confidence that if any of the battered souls could be saved, I was equal to it. The insecurity, the fear of the unknown, and the fear of an insurmountable technical challenge had gradually diminished until they finally disappeared. Did I profit at the expense of the patients? Possibly, for now I was more technically adept, surgically mature, and emotionally satisfied. I felt pangs of guilt about that. I wondered if I was diabolical, a ghoul, some kind of monster to think like that.

That I was intercepting death on the doorstep was a fact. My sense that the decision back in Milwaukee a thousand years ago had been the right one was stronger than ever. It seemed evident that I had taken a chance and succeeded, and that to have saved many lives was my enormous reward.

The choppers drew closer. My colleagues streamed out of the officers' club and out of their quarters. The first Huey hove into view and landed.

A corpsman rushed up to me. "They've got one for you, LT," he said. "They say it's real bad, sir!"

I nodded and headed toward the shock Quonset.

The casualties kept coming, but as usual there were lulls. I found myself feeling very introspective during the quiet times. I guess that was natural. I wondered if my confidence and skill would be left behind in Vietnam, and I'd revert back to the man I was when I arrived.

Will I be a has-been?

I felt like I was about to be supplanted from an enormously gratifying medical and surgical experience mixed with adventure and personal danger. This was the paint and canvas providing an image and theme of a complex surreal mural that I was in the process of mentally painting. Ironically, I would never be able to complete that picture when I left China Beach.

A few days later, my emotional quagmire abruptly ended. I was standing in the sand near one of the Quonsets in which officers live, when one of my friends wandered by, carrying a football. I asked him if we could play catch, and he eagerly agreed. For the next thirty minutes or so we threw the football back and forth, practicing the fine art of passing. We began to hurl with greater force. During one of my catches, the ball struck directly on my outstretched left fifth finger, triggering a sudden sharp severe pain and shock sensation in my hand. The hand began to swell, and we both recognized that something more than a bruise had occurred.

With a shrug I headed over to the X-ray area, obtained a film of the left hand, and confirmed that there was a fracture. It was bad enough that a surgeon broke his hand, and it was even worse if it was his dominant hand. I knew my career in Vietnam was over. To make matters worse, there was no one to take my place.

One of the orthopedic surgeons examined my hand and advised me that it would require a cast. We both knew that would not be possible since there was no backup neurosurgeon in the area and casualties would continue to flow. No doubt some of them would be directed to me. We therefore compromised and agreed upon a splint secured with adhesive tape that immobilized my left hand. When a neurological operation was required, I would be able to remove the splint and somehow carry out the indicated procedure.

The accident was immediately reported to the commanding officer who, recognizing the magnitude of the problem, promptly sent a radio dispatch to the navy's Bureau of Medicine and Surgery in Washington, advising them of the urgency of an immediate neurological replacement. The commanding officer and I discussed the matter, and before he even told me, I was fully aware of the fact that it would take many days before another navy neurosurgeon would receive orders, be processed for combat field medicine, and then travel the necessary 12,000-plus miles to assume duty.

I told the commander that I had been working much of the time with the competent Dr. Ward Trueblood. I noted that with his help plus the use of an oversize sterile glove on my swollen left hand I could continue to function without degradation of performance. The navy hospital ship, which frequently roamed offshore, was presently not on station and apparently back in the Philippines. Since the ship was 1,000 miles away and she traveled about seventeen to eighteen miles per hour, no help could be expected in the near future from that source.

Over the objections of the orthopedic surgeon who warned that I may end up with a permanently crippled hand, the plan was decided upon. Necessity was the mother of invention, and as cases came in, I removed the tape and splint, and then assisted Ward, who knew from helping me previously how to surgically proceed through the scalp and the rigid cranial vault to enter the brain, at which point the much softer tissue of the brain and its coverings were managed by me. I used my right hand, augmented by the left thumb and index finger, to manipulate what is referred to as a "bayonet forceps," a common neurological instrument useful in this type of surgery.

After each case, I would put the splint back on my hand, again wrap it with tape, and wait for the next casualty. To say the hand was not painful during long surgical procedures would be a misstatement of fact, for the fractured opposed edges of bone in my hand during these surgical operations were literally grinding back and forth against each other. I did, however, use light pain medication before the surgery to afford some degree of comfort. Following surgery and after the hand was rewrapped, however, the pain usually subsided significantly and quickly. Ward and I continued in this mode for approximately two weeks, during which the replacement neurosurgeon completed his familiarization process in the United States and was sent over.

Ironically, when he arrived I was within one week of completing my twelve-month tour. Coincidentally, my replacement was Dr. Bill Parks, a young neurosurgeon with whom I had trained at the Mayo Clinic. Following the completion of his training, he too entered the navy and was stationed at the naval hospital in San Diego. He was married with two small children, and when he was told on an emergency basis that he was being sent directly to Vietnam, the emotional impact on him and his wife was quite dramatic, to say at the least. Apparently his wife was quite angry at me.

Evidently he had not been the neurosurgeon who was designated to replace me and, thus, was totally astounded at his sudden change in fortune. Fortunately, we were very good friends, and when we met after his arrival he greeted me in a pseudo-sarcastic manner with the remark, "Damn it Paul! Can't you behave yourself!"

Over the next few days we were constantly together so that I could orient him to the hospital procedures and practice patterns. I outlined as accurately as I could the various types of trauma he could expect to see and then advised him that, as they came, I would assist him at surgery so that before I departed he could have accrued as much hands-on experience for this type of trauma as was feasible.

About four or five days after Dr. Parks arrived, I was told that my orders were ready and I was to board a plane the following day for return to the United States and that, after a thirty-day period for furlough, I would be assigned to the naval hospital in San Diego for my second year in the navy.

Even though I was aware that I could no longer adequately function as a neurosurgeon at China Beach, I was beset with the notion of reticence to depart. After a year of carrying out the surgical procedures I had trained so long for, I was replaced.

Indeed, I had gone through enough emotional swings to make a psychiatrist seasick. For certain, I felt that I had made an impressive contribution to many wounded young men and obliquely to society. I matured as a surgeon, perceived enablement as a man, and established meaning to my life.

Regrettably I was of the mind that nothing on earth could compare to these feelings of attainment. All events and encounters later in life and career would be of an anticlimactic nature. Never again would I be chosen to stand between so many injured people and a graveyard—truly a challenge and responsibility of enormous proportions by any standard.

What would I do from this point hence to even remotely approximate the elation and exhilaration I perceived by being so needed? I obviously could not answer such a rhetorical question at the time. Now, more than forty-five years later and at the end of a long professional career, I can answer the question. I was right to feel the way I did. I never again felt as needed. There is nothing like Vietnam!

When the day of my departure came, I wandered off to my rack in the officers' housing Quonset and began to assemble the limited items with which I came. I easily packed them into the same seabag I used to carry all my belongings to this land. I continued to conjecture and predict in an attempt to plan my future. Remorse set in over the fact that I would no longer be a factor in the greater scheme of surgery I knew so well. My thoughts drifted back in time, and I again pondered the bigger questions I had grappled with during the past year. I looked deep into myself, seeking answers I did not have. I could only retrace the ground I had already covered.

To study medicine and neurosurgery so long, and yet be aware that the skill I had learned was by no means mastered upon my arrival in Vietnam, was immensely frustrating. That knowledge haunted me night and day at Charlie Med, and for very good reason. My lack of skill had tragic consequences in some cases. Ultimately, I rose to the occasion. I acquired the skill because I had to. I wanted to. If I didn't, men would die, or worse, they'd be turned into vegetables when they might have had a fighting chance under the hand of a surgeon with more experience.

To face all this with no thought or expectation of money or material gain I believe most closely approaches the lofty and altruistic goal for the pursuit and the practice of medicine. That was the truth of what I had done, and I held that truth close. I embraced it.

If only I could be frozen in time! If only I could do it all again! I thought.

Presently, a marine driver appeared at the door of my Quonset and said, "Sir, I am here to carry your bag and escort you to the front gate. There is a vehicle waiting there to take you to the Da Nang Air Base."

I quickly lurched out of my reverie and stuffed the remainder of my belongings into my seabag, which except for the numerous surgical records and research data was no bigger than a year ago. I handed it to the driver and walked with him to the jeep. I said good-bye to various colleagues and corpsmen alike as we drove slowly toward the gate, where the hospital commander was waiting for us next to another jeep. We pulled up, and he handed me my set of orders and then shook my hand and wished me well. This was a war zone. There were no elaborate celebrations surrounding any physician's departure.

The driver and I got into the vehicle and drove down the now-familiar dusty road with its staggered checkpoints toward the Da Nang River, over the pontoon bridge with the sullen-faced marines still spaced many feet apart, and firing upstream at potentially lethal lily pads. One hundred times I had crossed this bridge, with its ear-deafening rifle fire. I now heard for the last time the repeated bark of gunfire as the jeep rumbled across the pontoon bridge, sensing the diminished noise as we headed for the airfield. It was like I had died and the ceremonial rifle squad was saluting.

I have evolved from a child to a man, and from a neophyte to a surgeon, I thought.

As we bounced over the dusty road and through the armed gate at the air base, I returned the salute of the rifle-laden guards and then watched as we drove along parallel rows of the now-familiar F-4 Phantom jets perched like hawks in their revetments. We proceeded another 1,000 yards and stopped near one of several olive-drab single-level buildings that represented the air terminal. The driver stopped the jeep and lifted my baggage out while I jumped out of the other side. He then came around behind the vehicle, put the baggage in front of me, rendered a salute, and then drove away.

It was the same airfield where one year ago I had climbed off a freight plane, found out that the hospital I was assigned to had been blown up, and felt like an abandoned orphan.

That day I was lonely and scared. On this day, I was just lonely.

Presently I was notified that the freight plane I was assigned to was heading to Bangkok, Thailand. I would then transfer to a larger air force plane going via Asia to the United States. I picked up my stuffed khaki bag and walked out over the tarmac to the plane, which this time was considerably bigger than the C-123 that had brought me into Da Nang.

I climbed in the side doorway and saw a pile of freight. Clearly, I was going out the same way I came in! I turned around, and I took one last look at the country that had brought about so many changes in my life. At that moment, it occurred to me again that I was probably one of only a few who were leaving this place with such little personal jubilation. Gone were Bart Bean, Ward Turner, and Walter Bancroft. Gone were Captain Canada, Len Williams, and Jerry Long. Gone were so many of the other people I'd met at Charlie Med and at China Beach who played a part in my transformation. Life had given me a window of time to know, like, and respect these men, with their diverse characters, their cohesive cooperative abilities, and their rigid adherence to respect for mankind. However, life had also said, "That's enough!"

I turned away from the door and sat down among the numerous freight boxes. The door slammed shut, and I blinked to adjust my eyes to the dim light. The engines began to whine. I smelled exhaust. As the plane taxied and accelerated, its wheels lifted off from the blood-soaked soil of Vietnam, and I closed my eyes and felt the first intriguing tug of the future.

Addendum

A) Policy bone chip removal following Korean War
   Text:
   Neurological Surgery of Trauma
   Office of the Surgeon General
   Department of the Army, Wash. D. C.
   Page-117

B) Result of investigation during Vietnam Conflict
   Text:
   Journal of Neurosurgery Vol. 33 July, 1970
   Page-19

C) Present policy in Neurosurgery
   Text:
   Missile wounds of the Head and Neck, Vol.2
   AANS Publications Committee
   Page-272